COUPLES

HOW TO CONFRONT PROBLEMS AND MAINTAIN LOVING RELATIONSHIPS

Dr. Carlfred Broderick

SIMON AND SCHUSTER

NEW YORK

Published by Simon and Schuster
A Division of Simon & Schuster, Inc.
Simon & Schuster Building
Rockefeller Center
1230 Avenue of the Americas
New York, New York 10020
SIMON AND SCHUSTER and colophon are registered
trademarks of Simon & Schuster, Inc.

Designed by Stanley S. Drate
Manufactured in the United States of America
            7 8 9 10 11 12 13
Library of Congress Cataloging in Publication Data
Broderick, Carlfred Bartholomew.
    Couples: how to confront problems and maintain
loving relationships.

    Bibliography: p.
    1. Marriage.   2. Interpersonal relations.
3. Sex in marriage.   4. Marriage counseling.
I. Title.
HQ734.B838   301.42'7   78–11591
ISBN 0-671-43827-1

ACKNOWLEDGMENTS

First, I could not have written a book with such an optimistic view of marriage if it were not for the remarkable woman who has been my own partner for over twenty-five years. She is an inoculation against all world-weariness and skepticism that men and women were ever intended to be happy after the honeymoon.

Secondly, I am indebted to the hundreds of couples and individuals who have shared their lives with me over the years as clients and friends. I have drawn liberally upon what they have taught me, and where I have quoted them only discretion has kept me from giving full credit where it is due.

Thirdly, I have shamelessly drawn upon the wisdom of my colleagues who have written and lectured on this subject before. I am particularly indebted to Harry and Bonaro Overstreet for their development of what they called "psychic space" as a major determinant of behavior. Many of the best ideas in the book were borrowed from Richard Stuart, possibly the most creative marriage counselor I have ever known. For example, the use of behavioral contracts, of writing down and sharing positives about each other and instituting "caring days," and spelling out sexual and marital expectations in writing are all rooted in his work.

I am grateful to Albert Ellis for coining the word "horriblizing" and to David Olsen for its partner concept "personalizing," the twin assassins of emotional tranquillity.

Many have written about marital communication. I am almost reluctant to name those upon whom I draw most heavily lest others feel unjustly omitted. Some of the sources of which I am most appreciative are Carl Rogers, Bernard Gurney and Don Jackson. Others who see their pet ideas apparently borrowed without attribution will, I hope, be charitable.

Fourth, my secretary, Lynn Thompson, went beyond the call of duty and typed the first draft of this manuscript on overtime and between times. Beyond that, after each chapter she told me she liked it. I needed the encouragement.

Fifth, my agent, Don Cutler, has been more than an agent. His intelligent critique and creative suggestions have helped to shape the final form of the book.

Finally, I am tremendously indebted to Robert F. Capon, a professional writer and colleague, who has gone over the manuscript page by page and chapter by chapter. Somehow he has managed to tighten it, tune it up, enliven it without obscuring its original flavor or style.

CONTENTS

8   Contents

THE WAY YOU SAY IT IS IMPORTANT

Competitive Messages
Messages in the Supportive Mode
Exercises for Identifying Message Styles
    Identifying and Increasing Supportive Messages
    Identifying and Decreasing Competitive Messages

Differing Expectations
Core Symbols
Major Discrepancies in Life Scripts
Negotiating Improved Marital Scripts
    Instructions for "Wish List" Exercise
    An Optional Wish Form

Types of Resentment Hoarders
    The Hedgehog
    The Fox
    The Magpie
    The Mole
    The Bear
    The Hound Dog
Alternatives to Hoarding Resentment
Exercises
    Disengaging from Power Struggles
    Learning Assertiveness

COPING WITH DEPRESSION   126

Loss
Powerlessness
Boredom
Resentment Turned Inward

YOUR SEX LIFE   138

Sharing Sexual Scripts
Nondemand Pleasuring
    Nondemand, Nonsexual Pleasuring
    Nondemand Sexual Pleasuring
    Nondemand Pleasuring Including Intercourse
Special Exercise for Premature Ejaculators
    Learning Extravaginal Control
    Learning Intravaginal Control
The Kegel Exercise for Improving Vaginal Tone
Making Love Versus Having Sex

FIDELITY OR INFIDELITY?   156

The Case for Sexual Fidelity
Guidelines for Preserving Fidelity
    The Three R's of Infidelity:
    Resentment
    Rationalization
    Rendezvous
Surviving Infidelity and Growing from
    the Experience

REMARRIAGE   169

Triangles
    The Negotiated Solution
    The Imposed Solution
    The Philosophical Solution

INTRODUCTION

The most popular—and the roughest—contact sport in the country is not professional football; it is marriage. Consider the statistics: Over 90 percent of us try our hand at it, either ignoring the dangers or simply hoping for the best. A third of us, however, sustain so many injuries that we are willing to suffer the humiliation of divorce to get off the field. Yet the promise, the attractiveness, is so great that 80 percent of those divorced put themselves back into marriage—most of them within three years.

Clearly, the problem is not how to make matrimony more popular; it's how to make it less hazardous. This is a book to help you do just that. It comes out of twenty years of professional practice as a marriage counselor, and twenty-five years of private practice as a marriage partner. I write it in the conviction that the destructiveness and pain so many of us experience do not have to be the final word on the subject— that with guidance, most people can still make their marriages the joyful partnership they first hoped for.

In the natural course of events, though, marriages do indeed distribute themselves on a scale from marvelous to miserable. And it doesn't take long for the process to begin. After a single year of marriage, for example, approximately one-fourth of all couples have at least one partner who doubts that the marriage will succeed. The peak year for divorce is the third; and if the time needed to decide upon a divorce is taken into account, it is obvious that many marriages are in trouble from the very beginning.

However, while some find more and more disappointment as the months and years progress, others grow in love and vitality. Unhappily, the group that grows is in the minority. Even among marriages that survive the first twenty years, there is a powerful tendency for communication between mates to decline, interests to diverge, mutual criticism to increase and ardor to cool.

A study by J. F. Cuber and Peggy B. Harroff of four hundred occupationally successful men and their wives found that after fifteen to twenty-five years of marriage, they had sorted themselves into four groups, ranging from the happiest to the unhappiest.

VITAL. Only about one-sixth thought of their relationship in a way that could accurately be described as vital—that is, conceived of themselves as still having an active affectional and sexual life, as sharing significant interests and activities, and as positively enjoying their common life. For this group, marriage was viewed as a central and richly rewarding part of their lives.

CONGENIAL. These couples—one-third of the sample—lacked the vitality and the energetic involvement of the previous group, but still rated themselves as happily married. They took it for granted, however, that their relationship would fade rather than flourish over the years. They demanded little of each other and met most of their personal needs by occupying themselves with children, friends or work. Yet for all that, they described each other as pulling a fair share of the load, and felt loyalty and affection for their partners.

DEVITALIZED. This group, also about one-third of the whole, looked back on an earlier period of vitality with nostalgia—and with a tinge of bitterness that it was now over. Outwardly, they enjoyed the reputation of having a successful marriage. In fact, they were sometimes embarrassed at being held up as models of happiness when they themselves felt empty and resentful. On balance, they probably had about as much interaction as the Congenial group, but they felt differently about it. They tended to believe, cynically, that all apparently happy marriages were as empty as their own. They stayed together for practical reasons; children, a prosperous life-style, the good opinion of relatives and friends, the lack of attractive alternatives. They were reluctant to part with the image of vitality, even though its substance was gone.

COMBATIVE. This group, the unhappiest sixth of the couples interviewed, were locked in continual conflict and power struggles. Rarely did they show affection or support for each other except, possibly, for public show. Their combativeness was restrained somewhat in order to preserve the externals of the marriage, but it was precisely hurt and anger that were at the core of their emotional relationship.

I assume that different readers will find themselves in different categories. You may have a vital relationship you want to preserve and enrich; or you may have a congenial, or a devitalized one you wish to infuse with new life; or you may have a combative union you want to reshape altogether. In any case, the principles of marital growth outlined in this book should prove helpful to you. My aim is practical: to provide a book that couples can use on their own to achieve appreciable results in a short time. And my thesis is correspondingly simple: marital growth, as I conceive it, comes from increasing the amount of personal support each partner feels from the other, and from decreasing the number of put-downs and disappointments received.

Put as plainly as that, it sounds as if it should be easy

to achieve: each one simply decides to be nicer to the other, and, presto!—results! (Actually, that works more often than not. I recommend trying it.)

Sometimes, though, it seems that the harder you try, the worse things get. After weeks, or even months and years, of frustration, the conclusion most people come to is that the problem lies in the character deficiencies of their spouses. If only their partners weren't so lazy or selfish or uncaring or stupid or immature or oversexed or frigid or under the evil influence of their mothers ... then perhaps there might be hope. Others come to the less popular but still common conclusion that the deficiencies lie in themselves—that they are the ones who are unforgivably crazy, unattractive or dumb.

The trouble with both of these assessments is that there are no known cures for any of the conditions listed. It follows that nothing but further discouragement and resentment can result from such diagnoses. What is needed is a new diagnosis —one that fits the case, but suggests a cure as well. It has been my experience that the key to resolving a problem is learning to look at it in a new way. Find the right perspective and the solution fairly leaps out at you.

The chapters that follow aim at providing you with such perspectives on a number of common—and not so common— problems.

For example:

• How can I cope with feeling overwhelmed and trapped by my marital responsibilities, and how can I avoid making my partner feel that way?
• How can I let my partner know how I really feel without getting into quarrels, and how can I learn to better understand my partner's feelings?
• How can I avoid those vicious circles in which the harder I try to make the marriage better, the worse everything gets?
• How can I deal with anger and depression (mine and my partner's) without destroying my marriage in the process?

• How can I help to make money and children and in-laws and sex into issues that unite instead of divide us?
• How can I avoid infidelity—or if it has already occurred, how can I deal with it constructively?

The principles discussed are liberally illustrated with material from couples whom I have counseled over the years. There are also exercises to develop the skills and habits you need to solve the redefined problems.

And finally—since the old patterns of interaction are sometimes so entrenched that outside assistance is called for—there is a "Consumer Guide to Marriage and Sex Counselors" to help you choose from the often bewildering array of "helpers" available.

This book is absolutely guaranteed to provide you with penetrating insights into everyone else's marriage and how it could be improved. It is almost certain to sharpen your awareness of how much your partner could improve the relationship with a few well-chosen changes. With a little luck, you may also find an idea or two that will cause you to rethink your own marital behavior. If even one of these ideas leads to new approaches which result in your marriage's becoming more the way you hoped it would be when you signed the wedding certificate, I will feel satisfied that I have written a useful book.

1

SPACE ENOUGH FOR LOVE

Scene: *Jack and Margie over coffee after dinner.*

MARGIE ... but what is it you want me to do that I don't do already?

JACK Well, you brought it up: I just wish you were more feminine. That's very important to me.

M. What do you mean, "more feminine"? I'm a woman; how can I be more feminine than that?

J. I mean *act* more feminine.

M. You want me to wiggle my hips when I walk?

J. Margie, grow up.

M. No, really, what do you want? You want me to giggle and blush? To wear flimsy negligées and perfume? I don't know what you're talking about.

J. Look, I'm sorry I mentioned it. If I have to explain it in exact detail, forget it.

M.   How can I forget it when you say it's so important? Are you saying you want me to quit work and have a baby?

J.   Margie, you know I don't mean any such thing. The quality of true femininity is subtle and apparently beyond you, so let's forget it. (Exit)

Scene: Margie on the phone later.

. . . and then he just gets up and leaves. Honestly, Janice, it's as if he's tying me up with invisible cords. When he gets going like that, I feel trapped. All I want to do is get away—to escape to somewhere I can breathe.

THE PRINCIPLE OF EMOTIONAL SPACE

The words people use to describe their feelings when things are going badly are often clues to what makes marriages prosper or suffer. They use phrases which, taken literally, refer to their having run out of space. They complain of feeling crowded, cornered, trapped, in a tight spot. They send frantic messages that they're drowning, suffocating or being crushed. Clearly, it is an emotional, not a physical reality they describe.

Similarly, when people speak of a weight's being lifted, of being unburdened, of getting out from under, of breathing again, it's a gain in emotional, not physical, space that they're referring to. Anyone who listens to people talk about their problems could collect a large number of such phrases in a few hours. But what is it exactly that people are trying to communicate when they compare their situation to a lack of space? An analysis of such expressions suggests that two basic feelings are predominant.

First, these phrases imply a feeling of impotence, of inadequacy, of being overwhelmed by circumstances. Apparently, this loss of a sense of control and competence is experienced as a diminishing of their emotional room to maneuver.

Second, these terms express a feeling of lost options, of restricted alternatives. In particular, it appears that such valued and desirable roles as loving, forbearing, supporting, understanding or creating have been forced out of the repertoire of social responses. Emotional claustrophobia has left them with a choice of only two parts to play: that of the fighter, or that of the escape artist.

The vicious circle that results is familiar to everyone. Something happens to one of the marital partners to make him feel incompetent or unvalued. This is experienced as a loss of emotional space, with the result that his tendency to fight or run increases. But that in turn restricts the other's room to respond. In many marriages this pattern reaches a state in which they both live in emotional straitjackets all the time. Even in the best of marriages, however, the careful preservation of one's own and one's partner's emotional space is crucial to success.

We can best perceive the nature of emotional space by looking at what destroys it. Let us suppose, therefore, that I were determined, like a villain in a melodrama, to reduce my partner's space as much as possible. Taking my cue from the various words and phrases used to describe emotional claustrophobia, I could pursue a combination of three strategies.

1. Some of the phrases refer to being overwhelmed by more pressures than one can cope with (snowed under, swamped, buried or drowning in work, hemmed in on all sides, etc.). Therefore, one diabolically effective thing I could do would be add to his or her burden by increasing my expectations and demands, and, at the same time, withdrawing any help I might formerly have given. Even a well-organized and competent person will finally reach the point at which a single additional demand will exhaust her space and "drive her to the wall." If, by chance, my spouse is not very well organized or particularly self-confident, this is an especially easy and effective way to hem her in.

2. Other phrases imply that people are being pressed not by

too many expectations, but by *unclear* expectations—demands that leave them stymied about what to do (being in a bind, uptight, tied up in knots). These suggest a technique requiring even less effort than the first one. I don't need to hit my spouse with a lot of expectations; just one will do if I make it very clear how much the demand matters to me, but leave it very unclear exactly how it might be satisfied.

Consider the dialogue between Jack and Margie with which I began. The kind of vitally important, but ultimately ambiguous, demand he makes imposes on her emotional space to a degree quite out of proportion to the issue involved. If you think of the many demands of the first strategy as being a volley of arrows coming at a person from every quarter, then this strategy is a spear that pierces to the center of her personal space and pins her down with a single thrust.

3. Finally, some of the phrases suggest a still more direct strategy (crushed, deflated, put down, like I just got run over by a steamroller). In this approach you avoid the unnecessary middle step of laying impossible expectations on your spouse in order to make him or her feel inadequate. You make her feel bad directly by pointing out how incompetent she is—or better still, by saying nothing and treating her as if her incompetence were self-evident. In the dialogue above, for instance, Jack's exit line—and the exit itself—are excellent examples of this approach.

With the right combination of these strategies, even a saint can be driven out of emotional space in short order. It's time, therefore, to look more closely at how people behave when they have run out of emotional space.

The fundamental principle of emotional space has already been intimated:

As emotional space approaches zero, one's repertoire of social responses is reduced to two: fighting or running.

Of course, there are many ways to fight and many ways to run. Some fight literally and physically, punching noses or throwing crockery. Others fight verbally, with loud voices and four-letter words—or more cunningly, with sarcasm or nit-picking criticism. Then again, one of the most effective ways of fighting is not to fight at all, but simply to withhold what the other person wants or needs—to use passivity as the chosen means of aggression. Very often sexually impotent husbands or nonresponsive wives, lazy or late or absent-minded spouses are fighting back in their own fashion against partners who rob them of their emotional space.

Individuals sometimes rise to heights of ingenuity in their expressions of hostility. I will never forget a woman I knew in Minneapolis some years ago. One evening her car was in the shop and her husband forgot to pick her up after work. She waited forty-five minutes for him on a windy corner at 27 degrees (Fahrenheit) below before she finally was able to flag a cab. In similar circumstances any wife might be expected, on her return home, to yell at her husband, chew him out, sulk, slam doors, burn his dinner or refuse him sex for a week. Not this lady. She went directly to her sewing basket, took out a shirt of his that had been lacking a button for several weeks and sewed it on. She then presented it to him with a moral stinger: "Now, that's the difference between you and me."

In my view, that's class. But it's still only one of a thousand ways to fight.

Similarly, there are a thousand ways to run. Some people flee physically. We used to have neighbors who apparently did all their quarreling late at night. Every few weeks we would be awakened at about 2 A.M. by slammed doors, the roar of a motor and the screech of tires spinning on the gravel.

Someone was exercising the running option. But there are many other ways to run. Some run to television or to reading, to movies or to fantasy. Some run to alcohol or drugs. My own favorite escape happens to be sleep. Let my wife bring up some financial tangle I can't see my way through, and I am sound asleep in minutes.

But whatever form it takes, a person who is out of emotional space finds that his or her options are indeed reduced to fighting or running. Excluded are all warm, loving, understanding, constructive, creative, positive responses. Therefore, if you seriously want any of these supportive responses from your spouse, it follows that you need to help him or her maintain plenty of emotional room. Admittedly, adequate space alone can't guarantee good responses; but it does at least permit them. On the other hand, one can guarantee that no positive responses will be possible at all if the partner is constantly deprived of room.

Let me vivify that by an example. The time is six o'clock. The young husband arrives home to find the following scene: the rice is burning on the stove, the baby is crying, the three-year-old is yelling for a snack, the puppy has committed an indiscretion in the middle of the living-room rug and the telephone is ringing. The young wife's space is clearly under attack.

When I present this situation to classes, I always begin by asking, "Now, if for some reason the husband wanted to drive his wife's emotional space clear to zero—to leave her with absolutely no possibility of responding to him with anything but fighting or running—what might he do?"

Predictably, class responses fall into two categories: they suggest either adding arrows—that is, making further demands on her—or putting her down directly. (The third possible category doesn't apply: the situation is so supercharged that unclarity is not an issue; additional demands of any degree of clarity are too much.)

Class responses: Additional demands.
> Ask her when dinner is going to be ready.
> Tell her the phone is ringing or point out the dog mess.
> Ask her to fix him a drink.
> Tell her he is in a hurry.
> Tell her he brought home an unexpected guest.

Class responses: Direct put-downs.
> Yell at her for letting the puppy into the living room.
> Criticize her for not teaching the children that they shouldn't ask for food before dinner.
> Point out that something seems to be burning on the stove—and add, "So what else is new?"
> Suggest that he ought to get his secretary to come over and show her how to organize her time.
> Sit down in a chair and read the newspaper while she tries to cope with the situation.

I feel that any one of the above, let alone any combination of them, would be enough to guarantee fighting or running behavior from even the most resourceful and saintly wife.

But suppose now that he was motivated (whether selfishly or not doesn't really matter) to give his wife enough space so that she had at least the option of warm, positive responses. What could he do?

The most obvious answer is that he could answer the phone, or clean up after the dog, or do anything else that would intercept the arrows one by one. It is instructive to note the following class responses from males, and to compare them with some of the replies they provoke from females.

MALE SUGGESTION   I'd ask if there was anything I could do to help.

FEMALE CRITIQUE   If you can't see what has to be done, forget it.

In this kind of crisis situation, even an offer of help can seem like another arrow—just one more thing to be dealt with by someone who's already overwhelmed.

MALE SUGGESTION   I'd come up to her, kiss her and tell her she's beautiful and that I love her.

FEMALE CRITIQUE   Not now! First help me get out of this mess; *then* tell me all that good stuff.

The first order of business in this crisis is reducing the demands. Many women say that under these circumstances, they would interpret the affectionate approach as at best weak medicine and at worst an additional arrow. In a less embattled situation, the direct expression of affection might be appreciated; here it only intensifies the pressures.

MALE SUGGESTION   I'd take the whole crew to McDonald's.

FEMALE CRITIQUE   When things are going wrong, the last thing I want is for my husband to come home and say, "Well, I see you've blown it again. Never mind. Super-husband is here. I will rescue you all and take you out for hamburgers." That's just the ultimate put-down.

QUESTION FROM C.B.   What should he do, then?

FEMALE ANSWER   Sit down, shut up and eat what's put in front of him!

It must be admitted that not all females resent being rescued in this fashion, but it is important to note that if the offer of help is perceived as a put-down, rescue attempts backfire.

In this example, the crisis of emotional space was readily apparent. All of the arrows were obvious and had to be dealt with immediately. Often, however, this is not the case. A husband, for example, may be at the very end of his endurance, but the arrows or ambiguities or put-downs have occurred elsewhere—on the job, perhaps. Often the fighting or running itself (or at least the absence of any warm behavior) is the first evidence that your mate is in a tight spot. The danger here is that you will erroneously assume that your spouse is angry with you for something you did or failed to do. This may very well close out your own emotional space, making your response defensive or even aggressive. In this situation, it is easy to get into a series of exchanges in which each reduces the space of the other until truly hurtful things are done and said. In marriage counseling, husbands and wives frequently tell each other not to take everything so personally. As one man said, "I don't mean it as a put-down, but frankly, you're the least of my problems."

When one sees the danger signals, the first thing that is called for is simple supportiveness and perhaps a little creative listening as spelled out in the next chapter. Life is complex, of course, and it is true that complex problems often demand complex solutions; but attentive patience at least won't make the problem worse.

Nevertheless, if the Law of Emotional Space is fully understood, there are often quite simple remedies for apparently insoluble problems. I suggest that we make a list of the claustrophobic horror-chambers most frequently built by husbands and wives, and then spell out some of the things they can do to help each other enlarge their emotional space and increase their capacity for positive responses.

HELPING YOUR SPOUSE INCREASE HIS OR HER EMOTIONAL SPACE (and thus be free to be nicer to you)

Case 1: A crisis has developed. Your spouse is under enormous pressure from every quarter. Deadlines are creeping up inexorably, expected help has failed to materialize, there is simply not enough time or energy or self to go around. As a result, he or she is short-tempered, hypercritical, unaffectionate and downright impossible to live with. Most of us, under these circumstances, get to feeling annoyed and resentful ourselves and are likely to let it be known (thus increasing pressures). Understanding the principle of emotional space suggests effective alternative strategies. Below are a few suggestions that occur to me, but you may think of even better ways of helping your mate out of the bind.

- Pitch in and help where possible.
- Mobilize others to help (children, friends, relatives), if this can be done without offending your spouse. If the means are available, temporary paid help can sometimes be a lifesaver. Often people do not realize that high school and college youths will do a lot of work for a reasonable wage—not to mention professional typists, baby-sitters, carpenters, tax consultants, gardeners, housekeepers or accountants, who, for a perhaps more unreasonable wage, will still help your spouse keep his or her sanity.
- Review your own expectations for your spouse's behavior and see if some of them can be relaxed for the duration of the emergency. Let the lawn grow, the dust collect, the personal service or attention you hope for be temporarily forgone.
- Help him or her make a complete list of the self-imposed pressures which are so impossible to handle. Give special attention to those which might be postponed or renegotiated or even dropped altogether. Conscientious spouses often need a little support before they can get the courage to say "no" to others. It is important, however, that your support in this direction not become just another pressure. The person who lacks emotional space needs to feel sure that the decisions are his own and that no one is pushing

him into something he doesn't want to do. Otherwise, your attempt to help may just explode in your face.

- If you are well organized yourself, your spouse may appreciate specific help in organizing the things that must be done in order to reduce the chaos to manageable proportions. Ranking things in order of importance, or in order of difficulty, is often helpful. Allocating a certain amount of time or money or space to each task in advance sometimes works. But again, as in the previous instance, the offer of help should not be coercive.

- Help your husband or wife to take a breather from the situation. Go to a movie, take a walk, do something relaxing and unrelated to the problems. This does nothing to reduce the number of arrows, of course; but it does get the spirit off the archery range for a little refreshment so that the same pressures may seem less overwhelming.

Case 2: It doesn't take a crisis to put your spouse out of emotional space. He or she seems to feel hassled, overworked, on the run and behind all the time. As a result, you feel that you can never compete with this multitude of worries.

This is a difficult case for three reasons. First, being on the run is often a lifelong habit, and therefore difficult to break. Secondly, either you or your spouse (or both of you) may actually have come to admire hyperactivity and to place a low value on leisure, or on being kind to oneself. Third, life itself sometimes offers few alternatives. A mother of young twins, for example, or a husband who has two jobs, or a couple who both work full time are, by definitions of their situations, liable to be chronically out of emotional space. Nevertheless, the suggestions listed below are often helpful, even under such inevitable pressures.

- Consider reevaluating the division of labor between you. Perhaps the expectations you brought to marriage do not fit your situation very well at this point. The one with more

space may be able to relieve the other of obligations that
have become oppressive.

• Help your partner reevaluate the division of labor between
himself and other important people in his life. Often great
inequities develop which nevertheless can be set right once
a serious case is made from doing so. This may be true not
only at home but on the job, or in religious or social or-
ganizations. With support, the overaccommodating and
overworked partner can often make substantial redefinitions
of what is a reasonable contribution in various settings.

• Encourage your spouse to consider refusing obligations that
actually do not represent major value commitments. No one
can be everything to everyone.

• Support your spouse by urging regular time off from present
obligations. For example, a mother with young children
may need to take one day a week off to pursue adult needs;
an executive may need to get away with his family from
time to time. Constant expenditure of energy must be
matched by regular intake of nourishment.

• Sometimes just listening attentively while your spouse talks
out frustrations helps facilitate a breakthrough to one of the
solutions above.

Case 3: Your spouse constantly complains that he or she
just doesn't understand you, has almost given up trying to
figure out how to please you, and accuses you of being un-
appreciative and impossible to satisfy.

In this case the only solution is to be very specific in communicating what you want. The next chapter goes into the
matter of clear communication in detail, but it is often helpful simply to ask yourself: What would I accept as compelling
evidence that my spouse was doing a good job of meeting my
expectations? Then it is usually a good idea to think of something equally compelling that you could do to demonstrate
your own affection and concern.

One creative therapist, Richard Stuart, uses the technique of giving poker chips to the spouse whose expectations are seen as unclear. This partner is then given instructions to give the other a blue chip when something appreciated is done, a white chip for a good try that just doesn't come off, and a red chip for something that definitely is not appreciated.

One case in which the technique worked involved a man who claimed he had no idea what his wife wanted and could never please her. She was given charge of the chips with instructions to carry them in her purse and give one to him every time he either pleased her, tried and missed, or displeased her. After some hesitation she agreed. The following week, the man reported two incidents that he felt had revealed to him a completely unexpected aspect of his wife's personality.

On the weekend between sessions, they had gone to a party and both had had a bit too much to drink. As the party progressed, the husband became increasingly annoyed at his wife's conversational involvement with another man, and especially at the man's evident enjoyment of the view she gave of her breasts every time she leaned forward to talk with him in the noisy room.

Finally, the husband became so upset that he interrupted the conversation and curtly told her they were going home. As he gunned the car out of the driveway she asked him what on earth had gotten into him. He told her that it made him sick to see the way she was showing off everything she had. She asked him to pull over to the curb and put on the car lights so she could get him a token. He cursed under his breath while she fumbled in her purse in the dim light, but finally, when she gave him a blue chip, he exploded: "You're so damn drunk you can't tell one color from another. You want a red chip; this is a blue one." She said, "Nope, you get a blue one." "Why?" "Because at least you told me what you were mad about. Usually you'd pout for a week and slam doors and I would never be able to find out exactly what it was all about." He said, "Well I'll be damned."

The second occasion was on the evening they were to have their counseling appointment. In trying to get off on time she had not kept a close eye on the meat loaf, and it was over-cooked. Despite this, he went out of his way to compliment her on the meal. She stalked off and brought him back a red chip. "Red? For complimenting you on the dinner?" She said, "You know very well the meat loaf was dried out. You were just trying to collect chips to impress the doctor!"

After a couple of weeks of this, he began to be able to guess her feelings correctly nearly all the time. The ambiguity in their relationship had been replaced by mutual understanding.

If you are a couple who enjoy a playful approach to a problem, the Poker Chip Ploy might be one way to clarify ambiguous expectations.

Case 4: Your spouse feels down. The complaint is that nothing ever goes right: "There's no use trying; the harder I try the worse things get."

- Show affectionate concern. Do not try to talk your spouse out of the feeling; above all, never label the behavior as foolish or unwarranted. In these circumstances, nothing works better than good listening and physical consolation.

Case 5: Your spouse has a chronically negative self-image and consistently feels inadequate and unworthy.

- Systematically support and show appreciation for your spouse. Be sure that your efforts are on target and sincere.
- If your own efforts are not effective, consider consultation with a competent counselor. (See Chapter Thirteen.)

Case 6: Independently of any special pressures, your spouse is habitually ill tempered, abusive and inconsiderate.

This is a very difficult case. The symptoms are strongly suggestive of a chronic lack of emotional space based on a low self-image. I am aware of only one strategy forceful enough to have any hope of success.

• Administer a heavy, continuous dose of positives—praise any traits you can find to praise, support any desirable behavior as enthusiastically as possible—for at least three weeks. He or she may not much deserve such treatment, but it is powerful medicine, and hard to resist.

INCREASING YOUR OWN EMOTIONAL SPACE

Sometimes, however, there just is no one around to help you regain your lost space. You have no partner, perhaps, or your partner has a negative attitude toward self-help exercises —or is so out of space himself that he is in no shape to help anybody. For whatever reason, you find yourself alone in facing the work of enlarging your space. How do you go about it? Basically, by adaptations of the same rules that apply in the case of spouses working together.

Case 7: You feel overwhelmed with responsibility. You have said "yes" to too many people. There seems to be no possible way of getting everything done that needs to be done. You may feel so immobilized that you just sit and look at the mountains of work, unable even to begin a task you cannot hope to finish successfully.

• Determine your obligations and rank them according to priority. Some prefer to rank them in order of importance, taking care of the major ones first. I myself like to rank them in terms of the difficulty—or the satisfaction—they give me. Then I take the easiest or the most rewarding first. In this way my emotional space gradually expands as the tasks become more difficult; by the time I get to the tough ones, the room I need in which to maneuver is more than likely to be there. Whatever the strategy, though, developing a list or plan of attack is the first step. Even if the list itself is overwhelming, it may reveal the places where changes need to be made, responsibilities reduced or help obtained.

- Using the list you have just made, consider seriously the possibility of getting rid of some of your responsibilities by delegating, mobilizing help or simply resigning from the obligation.
- Take time out to meet your own needs, or at least to see them in perspective. Some people go out on a buying spree; others go golfing or horseback riding or to a movie. Some meditate; others pray. When Theodore Roosevelt felt overwhelmed by the pressures of office, he used to go out under the stars and contemplate the vast distances of the universe. He said that when he returned to his desk, his problems had been placed in perspective and assumed manageable proportions.

Case 8: You cannot seem to please the important people in your life. Each one pulls you in a different direction and none seems satisfied or appreciative even when you knock yourself out to please him. Often you feel like giving up. Perhaps in bleak moments you may even feel it would be a service to those you love just to leave or do yourself in. Then maybe they could find somebody who could meet their needs. Maybe they would even discover (too late) that not everyone would work as hard to please them as you have.

This is a particularly tough situation to break out of, because at least in my own case, I find self-pity has a cloying, perversely addictive quality that is hard to fight. If the problem of motivation can be licked, there remain two other aspects of the problem to be dealt with: learning to relate more effectively to the people in your social environment, and learning to depend less on the evaluation of others for your own sense of worth.

- Relate More Effectively. Learn to be a creative listener and a sender of clear messages. Don't let it be inattention or ambiguity on your part that is the cause of the problem (See Chapter Three.) Learn to safeguard the emotional space of the important people in your life so that you don't unintentionally push them into fighting or running.
- Learn to Be Less Dependent. Take responsibility for the solution of your own problems. Give up the luxury of blaming things on "them" (spouse, employees, children, parents, friends, even God). Acknowledge that while what happens to you may not be your responsibility, the way you respond to it is under no one's control but your own. This is a hard doctrine and may seem to contradict the Law of Emotional Space. It is based, however, on the assumption that no one's emotional space is ever reduced entirely to zero and that, therefore, there is always some choice of responses. It is important to own up to that possibility of choice. Doing so immediately increases one's emotional space, since it enlarges one's sense of control and competence.
- Accept the judgment of others as being of concern to you, but not as binding upon you. "I regret that you can't support me in this and I know you're sincere, but I'm doing what I feel I ought to do," or " I know it makes you feel bad that I won't be able to come and I'm sorry to cause you pain, but I've decided that I need to stay at home this time." If you are taxed with being "selfish," you can respond, "I know it must seem that way to you and I am sorry you can't see it differently, but I must do what seems best to me."

In all candor, this attitude is difficult to achieve if you are in the habit of deriving a sense of your own worth from the opinion of others. It may be helpful to seek short-term counseling if efforts to achieve these new ways of thinking are not successful.

Case 9: You feel depressed and worthless. You can't sleep through the night and can't get up when it is time to get up. Life tastes flat, stale and unprofitable to you.

I devote a whole chapter to this issue later in the book; but if the depression is not too deep, it might respond to simple home remedies such as:

- Be good to yourself. Look at yourself in the mirror at least three times a day and say, "I like you; you're a good man, Charlie Brown." It would also be helpful to list two or three good qualities each time in order to provide some support for the assertion.
- Spend some money on yourself for a pair of socks or a meal out—or for a phone call to Bangkok or a new Jaguar. Anything that won't break you will tend to make you.
- Do something for someone who doesn't expect it. If the opportunity offers itself, drown someone in praise, encouragement and help for six days in a row. Not only will you like yourself better, but you will increase the chances of getting more than a punch or a shrug in return.

However you do it, no advice given in this book is as likely to pay off for you as this: Protect the space in your marriage—leave room enough for the good things to happen.

The next several chapters are designed to help you develop the skills and habits that can place you in the championship class as a Space Preserver.

2

COMMUNICATING
EFFECTIVELY

HE   So what are you pouting about? Admit it, this was one of the great meals of all time.

SHE   (No answer.)

HE   Come on, this is our anniversary. Let's don't spoil it. Tell me what's bugging you.

SHE   (No answer.)

HE   It's what I said about the ice cream, right?

SHE   (Looks at him accusingly.)

HE   This is really too much. It's not enough that I knock myself out to fix a really superb meal—artfully seasoned, creatively presented. And what do I get from you? The suggestion that what we need for dessert is cherry-vanilla ice cream from the supermarket. I can't help it, that's the stupidest suggestion I ever heard. I might as well have cooked hamburger and French fries.

SHE   All right. All you had to say was you didn't want to serve ice cream! You didn't have to make me feel like I picked my nose in public. You have a way of making me feel so . . .

HE   Don't be disgusting. That is all I did say. I can't say anything to you without your making a federal case out of it. The trouble with you is you have to win 'em all. If I ever disagree with you on any point, you pout for ten days till I give in. Well, to hell with you. You can eat your cherry-vanilla ice cream for breakfast for all I care.

SHE   You are without doubt the most contemptible snob in the history of the world. It makes you feel great, doesn't it, to make me feel like a slob? Well I'll tell you this, I'm sick and tired of it. You hear me? (Shouting) I don't need it!

HE   (Shouting) I can't stand this! I can't stand not being able to open my mouth in my own house! Damn. Damn. Damn! (He punches a hole in the dining-room wall.)

SHE   (Screams and runs out of the room crying.)

So much for what started out to be a special first-anniversary dinner. The chef cooked his own goose . . . or was it her fault for not leaving the menu totally in his hands? Whosever fault it was, the resulting blowup seemed out of all proportion to the initial provocation.

This chapter is about the kinds of problems that arise because people either don't listen with sensitivity, or don't express their feelings effectively. Consider the exchange between the couple above: he hasn't really heard what she is trying to say about her feelings; she makes no effort to see his point of view; neither of them learns a thing about himself; and both are astonished that such an apparently trivial exercise in communication can end in so major a misunderstanding.

It isn't simply that they need to make clearer the things they are saying to each other. Clarity is, of course, an asset in most marriages; but there are many relationships which survive only because of a conspiracy to keep things foggy. If all a couple do is clear up their messages, they may have nothing left to deal with but such unvarnished truths as "I have never loved you," "Your body disgusts me" or "I'm having an affair with someone else."

Clearly, clarity isn't everything. What is needed is not so much clearer messages as clearer channels through which to hear and receive them—unjammed frequencies, as it were; better habits of listening and talking—so that even when something is badly said it still gets a good hearing, and even when something is misheard, there is at least a chance to hear it again without static's building up.

Clear-channel communication, therefore, is the product of two reciprocating factors: effective expression of intentions and feelings on the part of the sender, and creative listening on the part of the receiver. But since listening is the hardest technique to learn, it deserves the first consideration.

CREATIVE LISTENING

People everywhere have a longing to be listened to, but good listeners remain a rare and valued commodity. Realizing this, a widow I know decided to enliven her loneliness by placing the following public-service ad in the local papers:

> WILLING TO LISTEN
> Will not give advice
> or interrupt. Call ———

After one day she had her phone disconnected. The flood of pent-up talk seeking an ear to pour itself into simply overwhelmed her.

Of course, there is more to creative listening than just holding your tongue, but that's a big part of it. Between husbands and wives, it may well be the hardest part. It's one thing to keep your peace while listening to a stranger on a topic of no personal relevance; it's quite another to hear out your spouse on the subject of your own flawed character. Yet the discipline of doing so is fundamental, and until it is mastered, one can hardly be considered ready to acquire any of the more advanced interpersonal skills. No other technique can make up for a failure to just plain listen.

Take the couple at the beginning once again. When she comes out of her pout with the words "You have a way of making me feel . . . ," he simply doesn't hear what she's saying about feeling put down by him: he's too busy with his pent-up anger to listen. And when she's confronted with his real resentment (he feels she has to "win 'em all" and always does), she doesn't hear what he's saying either: by then, she's also too furious to listen.

The other part of creative listening is checking with your partner about your impression of what is being said. Failure to do this leads often to hurt and anger which might have been avoided had there been no misunderstanding. In the dialogue above, for example, the fury at the end is the direct result of not checking out impressions. He thinks she's talking about winning; she thinks he's talking about her inadequacies. But they're both wrong, and a settled habit of comparing notes before the pitched-battle stage is reached would keep their marriage—not to mention their walls—in better condition.

The results of incorporating these two aspects of good listening into a marital relationship are often astonishing. Yet we should not be surprised at the impact in view of all that is accomplished by these simple means.

1. The attitude of listening itself shows love, concern and respect. As we saw in the previous chapter, any act that expresses a positive attitude is likely to trigger a sequence of positive responses back and forth between husband and wife.

2. By the same token, the avoidance of interrupting and criticism prevents the sending of negative messages such as "I don't care how you feel or what you think," "You're not worth listening to." The speaker's emotional space is left open, and he's freed by the listener from the pressure to fight or run.

3. You discover how things actually look from your spouse's point of view. There's a risk, because what you hear may be surprising and even unsettling. But it is nearly always worth it. In fact, it's hard to imagine how any couple can become close without achieving insight into each other's feelings.

4. You lose your status as chief expert on what your spouse really thinks, wants, fears and feels. Instead, your spouse takes over as the final authority on his or her own feelings. In addition to restoring to each partner the inherent right to speak for himself, it may also have a valuable side effect. If you listen sympathetically to your spouse, he or she is able to develop a greater clarity in areas that may have been confused and confusing. In fact, creative listening is the technique used by counselors to help individuals sort out confusion in their own feelings.

5. You set an example for your spouse to follow in listening to your own feelings.

One of the assignments I give in conferences with couples is to ask husband and wife to attempt an exchange following these rules. Each in turn is to be first the sender and then the receiver of clear-channel communications. The sender's job is to choose a feeling that he believes has never been clearly understood by the partner. Perhaps it has never been expressed before, or perhaps it has been expressed hundreds of times; but in either case, the sender feels it has never been received with understanding.

In the next section of this chapter we will consider more fully what is involved in effective sending; but most often it is the receiving, not the sending, that snags couples when they attempt this exercise. Bad listening habits give them their biggest problems. Take, for instance, the following exchange —one that would be not at all unusual for the first try:

C.B.   Now. You understand the instructions. Who wants to be first?

WIFE   I do. There's one thing that we've talked about and talked about but I don't feel you've ever understood . . . *really* understood how I feel about it.

HUSBAND   (Warily) What's that?

WIFE   It's the way you embarrass me at parties by telling stories about me which you think are funny but which always make me look like a complete idiot.

HUSBAND   Oh, for heaven's sake, let's don't waste our time going over that stupid argument again.

WIFE   But we never settle it. I tell you how I feel and you go right back to the next party and do it again as though we'd never discussed it.

HUSBAND   Honey, you're too sensitive. They're just harmless little stories. Everyone enjoys them but you, and nobody—

C.B.   (*to husband*) Excuse me, but you are supposed to be listening to her expression of feelings without interrupting or criticizing.

HUSBAND   But she's being ridiculous, blowing this whole thing up out of proportion.

C.B.   When it's your turn you can express yourself fully on the subject if you choose; but right now your assignment is to try to get with *her* feelings.

HUSBAND   But her feelings on this subject are ridiculous!

WIFE   I knew this would never work!

C.B.   (*to wife*) Now, wait a moment. I'm sure your husband can get the hang of it with a little concentration. Now (*to husband*), can you check out with your wife how you think *she* feels on this matter—not your views but hers? Can you put yourself in her shoes and see how she feels?

HUSBAND Oh, I know how she feels.

C.B. Okay, but check it out. See if she agrees that you have it right.

HUSBAND She thinks I'm purposely trying to humiliate her at parties. Actually, I'm doing no such thing. If she weren't so supersensitive—

C.B. (*to wife*) Is that right? Do you feel he is purposely trying to humiliate you?

WIFE Actually, sometimes it almost seems that way. But no, I realize you don't see anything wrong with it. Yet you know it hurts me, and if you care anything for me at all, why do you continue to do it? (*Starts to cry.*)

C.B. (*to husband*) Try it again. See if you've got it this time.

HUSBAND Well, she...I know it hurts her, so why don't I quit doing it?

C.B. And what does she feel when you continue doing it?

HUSBAND That I don't love her.

WIFE I know you do love me, but it just seems to me that I'm not as important as your friends. You don't mind hurting me if you can make them laugh.

C.B. (*to husband*) Try it one last time. I think you've just about got it.

HUSBAND You feel that if I really loved you... cared about you...I wouldn't do something that embarrassed you ... even if I don't see anything wrong with it.

WIFE Yes!

HUSBAND (*quietly*) I'm sorry, honey. I know you didn't like it, but I really didn't understand till just now how it seemed to you.

C.B. Okay, good. Now it's your turn. Do you want to use it to explain feelings on this subject?

HUSBAND   No. Now that I see how she feels, well, I guess
I'll have to find something else to talk about at parties. . . .
But there is something I wish she could understand.

C.B.   Go ahead.

HUSBAND   Well . . . I work hard for my family, and as
I'm driving home fighting the rush-hour traffic, I'm thinking,
"Boy, will I be glad to get home where they love me." But
then when I walk in the door and yell, "Hi, everyone," it's
like dropping a stone down a bottomless well. The kids are
glued to the damned T.V. and don't even look up. You're out
in the kitchen getting dinner ready. Sometimes I have to
pinch myself to make sure I'm really there.

WIFE   Darling, I understand how you feel, but that's
the most hectic part of the day for me. The baby needs to be
fed and there are things on the stove.

HUSBAND   I really don't think you do understand how
I feel.

C.B.   (*to wife*) Why don't you tell him how you *think*
he feels and check it out with him?

WIFE   But the point is there is more to it than his feelings in this case. I'm just not free to drop everything and
welcome the Lord and Master home the way they do on T.V.
I have no help, just a hungry baby and—

C.B.   But in this assignment you don't have to do anything about it; you just have to try to understand how he
feels. Try it again.

WIFE   Well, he feels annoyed that the kids and I don't
drop everything we're doing and cater to him when he comes
in the door. Right?

HUSBAND   Marion, I don't . . . I realize how busy you are.
I just feel that if you were so glad when I get home as I am to
be there, you might at least acknowledge it somehow. I'd
settle for a kiss on the cheek. Hell, I'd settle for you poking
your head out of the kitchen and yelling, "Hi!"

C.B.   (*to wife*) Do you want to try again?

WIFE   He feels . . . (*turning to him*) you feel . . . that when you come home . . . after a long day's work and a long drive through traffic that . . . you'd like us to let you know we're glad you're home.

Husband   That's it exactly!

Wife   I am glad when you come home . . . but I guess I need to find a way to let you know it—even if it is the busiest time of the day.

It isn't always that difficult, but couples often have a hard time breaking old habits of communicating, especially bad listening habits.

EFFECTIVE SENDING

Probably the three most common barriers to communication on the sender's part are 1) refusing to communicate, 2) communicating in such an aggressive way that the listener is driven to a defensive position and 3) masking feelings behind intellectual analyses, projecting them onto the receiving partner and, in general, failing to be up front and straightforward about what is actually felt and thought.

The Non-sender. It is well to recognize at the beginning that there are many people in our culture who grew up in nonexpressive families. They not only have little skill in communicating feelings; they often think the whole idea of focusing on feelings is, to quote one gentleman, "a lot of damned foolishness." Then again, there are those whose resistance to communicating feelings grows in precise proportion to their spouse's efforts to get them to open up. The issue becomes a power struggle over when, where and how the reticent mate must be forced into self-expression.

Closely related is the spouse who is actually angry but who expresses that anger passively—by withholding affectionate and self-revealing communication. In effect, this behavior says, "You don't deserve to be my confidant because of what you've done (or failed to do) to me."

If any of these habits of refusing to communicate are deeply set in your marriage, it will not be profitable to attempt the exercise at the end of this chapter. The less communicative partner will simply feel (perhaps with some cause) bullied and badgered into doing something contrary to his best interests. Rather than feed that feeling, it would be better to proceed directly to the subsequent chapters which deal with some of the underlying causes of the reluctance.

THE ANGRY SENDER. In contrast to the spouse who refuses to communicate is the spouse who is quite willing to communicate feelings—but only angry ones, and only in the form of personal attacks. These assaults may be heavy-handed bludgeonings, with yelling and cursing, or they may be deft cuts with the scalpel of snide criticism; they may be frontal assaults or subtle ambushes from the rear; they may be couched in sour humor or in tears of rage or self-pity. What they all have in common is an attempt to "get" the other person, to stigmatize the partner as lazy, mean, sick, bad, selfish or inadequate. And as we have seen, it is extremely difficult to respond to an attack except by a counterattack or an escape from the field. Therefore, the first rule in any program of improving communication is that personal attacks, however disguised, are excluded.

This is not easy if one or both partners have been storing up resentments. In fact, the angry spouse may insist that any other response than an attack would be dishonest or hypocritical. He may even cite some pseudopsychology to the effect that he has to "get it out" or it will ferment and fester inside and make him sick. Or, his partner may hold that there cannot be an honest, open relationship unless each is free to "tell it like it is." As a young woman put it: "But I *am* angry . . . that's where I'm *at* . . . that's *me*. If you can't accept me as I am, if I have to become some simpering, saccharine, sugar-coated hypocrite before we can communicate, screw it!"

When confronted with this view, I never quarrel with a person's right to be angry. I am in no position to do so, since

I have not suffered the pain, humiliation, frustration or rejection that has caused the anger. But I do point out that while one person's anger may be fully justified, an attack on the other is not going to move the relationship in any good direction. It may make you feel better for a short time (although often it does not achieve even that), but after it's all over, the same task remains before you. Even this is not the whole truth; more accurately, it is the same task as before, plus the new hurt and resentment your partner feels because of the attack. And very often you find you have to deal with fresh angers inside yourself because the attacked partner countered with a still more hurtful response of his own.

It is my philosophy that people have every right to attack each other in this way; they should not, however, expect to reap anything from it except escalating resentment and pain. To improve the relationship, an entirely different approach is required—one that preserves the emotional space of the spouse. To reiterate, then: the first rule is to *avoid attack.*

There are two subrules for communicating about an issue over which resentment has accumulated. First, *stick to expressing your own feelings and resolutely avoid evaluating or criticizing your partner.* Suppose, for example, that your spouse hasn't phoned in to let you know her plans. What you should say is something like this: "When you don't let me know you're going to be late, I get very concerned about where you are and whether you're all right. Then when you do get home, I'm relieved that you're safe but still resentful that you seemed to care so little for my feelings." What you should not indulge in is a lecture on the state of your partner's moral development: "I don't see how, if you loved me, you could just let me sit there worrying for hours about whether you're in some ditch bleeding to death. You are totally self-centered and inconsiderate. You never think of my feelings at all."

These two outbursts may seem a lot alike, and they do indeed convey much the same information; but in the first example, the speaker sticks to stating his own feelings and doesn't paste derogatory labels on his wife. In the second case, his words can be taken only as an attack. A guilty person, of course, can read any comment as an attack; but with even a little goodwill, it is easier to listen creatively and empathetically to the first message than to the second. As we have seen, the first message permits the partner to step out of her own shoes and into the shoes of her spouse. It permits her to be understanding and compassionate. The second message puts her on the defensive and tends to evoke excuses, counterattacks or escape.

The second subrule for communicating successfully over a sensitive issue is to *avoid telling the other person how he or she feels.*

For a good example: "I hope we can find a way to avoid getting into a hassle with Mother when she comes this weekend. I know she has an opinion on everything, and it's easy to get offended by what she says; but it would mean a lot to me if somehow we could handle it so as to have a pleasant time." And, for an example of how to set up an instant Black Sunday: "I know you have never liked my mother and that you think it was stupid of me to invite her over for the weekend but . . ."

The first message states the problem from the viewpoint of the sender. The second message starts out by trying to state the problem from the viewpoint of the partner. The idea of seeing things in terms of your partner's perspective is a good one; but you can achieve it only by listening patiently and checking out your understanding. To assume you know what your partner feels not only robs him of his right to state his own case; it also makes you likely to be wrong. And that in turn gives him another problem: he now has to correct your misperception before he can discuss the matter: "It's not that I don't like your mother; it's just that . . ." In such cases it often happens that the original point gets lost in a snowstorm of arguments over who feels how about whom; what might have been a temperate weekend turns into an exercise in survival at forty below.

THE OBSCURE SENDER. For a variety of reasons, some people cannot express their feelings directly and simply. Often they are uncomfortable with their inward states because they consider them "bad": they feel resentment, anger, disappointment or sexual indifference, and they blame themselves for doing so, or they think that their feelings of need, pain or inadequacy are just one more proof of their constitutional "weakness."

In one workshop for couples, a young wife chose to explain to her husband why she didn't enjoy his touching her (it turned out that she had never forgiven him for "raping" her on their wedding night when she had wanted to wait). When it was his turn to express a feeling, he launched into a rambling lecture on the differences between men's and women's sex drives. It was hard for me to see exactly what he was getting at, but his wife finally had an insight and said to him, "Is this what you are trying to tell me: that my rejection of you on our wedding night was as deeply hurtful to you as the 'rape' was to me? I never even thought of that before this moment. I was so upset with how you made me feel, I never considered how I made you feel." Her husband looked at his shoes and said, "It's not easy for a man to say when he's hurting."

On another occasion, a young accountant took the first turn and expressed frustration at his wife's irresponsibility. He was especially offended that she sometimes wrote checks without recording them. He simply could not understand how a grown woman could be so irresponsible. She had no difficulty in reflecting his feelings accurately and did not seem upset by them, although they actually amounted to an attack on her. When it was her turn, she had a hard time thinking of something to share; finally, she started talking quietly about her feeling that although she was lucky to be married to such a strong and capable man, sometimes he seemed more like a father than a husband. He made her feel like a little girl.

HUSBAND   Don't blame it on me if you act like a little girl.

WIFE   I know it's my fault but . . . well, you never think my ideas are any good. Whenever I offer an opinion, you make fun of me. I did go to college for four years, you know. But you make me feel like a grammar-school dropout.

C.B.   (*to husband*) I know you want to defend yourself, but see if you can get at her feelings.

HUSBAND   You feel I treat you like a child.

WIFE   Yes. I know sometimes I do stupid things, but I'm getting such a complex about it that I can't even do simple things right when I'm with you.

C.B.   (*to wife*) How do you feel toward him for doing that to you?

WIFE   I know he has plenty of reason to, but—

C.B.   How does it make you feel toward him to be put in that position?

WIFE   I guess you want me to say it makes me mad, but that wouldn't be fair because it's mostly my fault.

C.B.   Maybe it wouldn't be fair, but is it true? Are you mad at him for making you feel incompetent?

WIFE   I know it's not right, but sometimes I get so angry I can hardly believe it's me.

HUSBAND   You never told me.

WIFE   I'm telling you now.

HUSBAND   Let me get this straight. You're mad at *me* because you're behaving in an irresponsible way?

WIFE   (*crying*) I'm mad at you because you always treat me so much like a child that I'm not even permitted to answer back. I'm not even allowed to get mad. (*louder*) Paul, I'm so stupid that the only way I can get back at you is writing checks and letting you try to figure out why the books don't balance.

C.B.   (*to husband*) You have a lot of information there. Let's see what you've absorbed. Check out with her your understanding of how she feels.

HUSBAND   You feel . . . angry . . . furious at me; only you don't think you have any right to . . . because I'm such a nice guy, right? . . . and because you don't have any good way, any way that I would accept as Okay . . . you do things that really get to me, like not recording checks. Is that right?

WIFE   Yes, except you left out the most important part . . . about your making me feel so stupid all the time.

HUSBAND   And the reason you feel so angry at me is because I make you feel stupid . . . all the time.

WIFE   Right! And even if it's true that I'm stupid, I don't think you have to point it out to me. . . . Besides, I'm really not stupid. My friends think I'm really quite smart. I got good grades in college. It's just with you I feel that way.

HUSBAND   I had no idea I did that to you . . . actually, that *we* did it to you. Anyway, whoever does it, we ought to get out of it.

Fortunately, their communication went on from that point, and they developed more satisfying ways of relating to each other. In this example I played an active role in helping the couple decode the obscure communication. Yet the husband might have done the same thing by himself if he had known what to look for. One basic rule of thumb in rooting out hidden feelings is to put yourself in the place of the other person and see how you would feel. In this case, I know that I would have felt angry at someone who consistently put me down. Certainly I would not have felt less angry if I partly deserved the criticism. In fact, out of frustration I might have felt worse. This knowledge about myself helped me have some idea about where to start in figuring out her emotions. In using this technique, however, it is imperative to check out such projections carefully lest one fall into the trap of arguing about how the other person really feels. Yet it can be a powerful tool in uncovering or clarifying obscured feelings.

Sometimes a person's experience in growing up has deprived him of the freedom to experience negative emotions. In such a case, a period of individual counseling may make it possible for him to get in touch with the forbidden, angry, fearful or sexually disreputable feelings behind the obscure communications. When it is realized that one can experience these feelings without acting on them (that is, without hurting, fleeing, seducing), it then becomes possible to discuss constructively the ways in which they are affecting the marital relationship.

CLEAR-CHANNEL COMMUNICATION EXERCISE

The exercise described below is similar to the ones used for illustration in the chapter. In this case, however, there is no counselor to bail you out if you run into difficulties. Most couples will find the exercise enjoyable and instructive. With practice, they may discover it to be a mode of communicating that will serve them well from this point on. Those with skill at generalizing their learning will also find situations beyond their marriage in which this technique can serve them. Clear-channel communicating cuts through the misunderstandings that jam many relationships.

There is much to be learned from the exercise, even if it is not entirely successful. Like several other techniques in this book, it has great diagnostic potential, often revealing to a couple just where the problem in their relationship lies.

It is not uncommon, however, for one partner to be enthusiastic about trying such an exercise while the other is resistant or even downright hostile to the idea. Even this gives valuable information to the pair and suggests several considerations. For example, perhaps the exercise—and even the whole "let's improve our marriage" bit—threatens to become just one more battlefield in a continuing power struggle over who is in charge of the marriage. If this appears to be so, the enthusiast should back off and reconsider the issue only after reading further in the book.

Another possibility is that partners may have come from different backgrounds and have different expectations of what marriage should be. One apparently has a scenario that stresses "growth" and "openness" (Which one of you bought this book?). The other may be looking for privacy and stability. One may be quite open to the kind of game-playing involved in this exercise, while the other will see it as a trifling approach to the grimly serious business of their relationship. Still others, like the ones in the examples referred to earlier, may discover that they need a referee at first. That is, they may find it difficult to keep the rules without a disinterested third party to help. Often a fair-minded friend or relative can serve if the couple feel comfortable with him. Or, two or three couples may work on this exercise together. While one couple are having their turn, the other couples act as arbitrators. I have seen children do admirably in this role, provided the subject matter was appropriate.

RULES FOR SENDER

1. Each partner chooses a message about a feeling he wishes the other to understand. It may have been discussed before or not.
2. Both agree on who is to have the first turn as sender.
3. The message should express the *sender's* feeling (using first-person statements as much as possible: "I feel," "I think").
4. The message must not be in the form of a direct attack on the partner; that is, it should not label the partner as

bad, sick, incompetent or selfish, although it may very well express feelings of hurt, disappointment or anger at what the partner does. The sender must steadfastly avoid speaking for the other person ("you feel," "you think").

5. The message should not be overly long or complex. When the listener has demonstrated understanding to the sender's satisfaction, his turn is over.

RULES FOR LISTENER

1. Do not interrupt, criticize, amend, contradict or comment upon the sender's message.
2. When the sender completes his or her first version of the message, check out your understanding of the *feeling* behind the message by asking, "Is this the way you feel . . . ?" or some equivalent question. The sender is the sole judge of whether you understood it or not, so listen carefully.

A couple may take as many turns as seems mutually profitable at a single sitting, but it is often best to start with only one or two rounds.

3

THE WAY YOU SAY
IT IS IMPORTANT

COMPETITIVE MESSAGES

A thirty-five-year-old divorcée and a forty-year-old bachelor met and, after a suitable courtship, decided to get married. As it turned out, he didn't own a suit to wear to the wedding. While this did not overly concern him, it did her, and she persuaded him without too much difficulty to go with her (in her car) to a men's shop to remedy the situation. When they entered the store, he proceeded to walk clear to the back toward a rack of suits with bright checks and stripes, and struck up a conversation with the salesman standing next to them. She stopped just inside the door at a rack of dark, conservative numbers. Finding one she liked, she looked up to get his attention and was horrified to see him apparently discussing brightly patterned suits with the salesman.

Unable to get his eye, she called to him in a voice he later described as "shrill, like a fishwife's" but which she said was "discreet": "Henry, not one of those; the ones you want to look at are over here." He ignored her, and in her annoyance, she called again: Henry, what can you be thinking? You can't get married in one of those. Now come over here and look at something sensible." Once more, he ignored her. "Henry, will you listen to me? I refuse to marry anybody dressed up like a vaudeville comedian." At this, he stalked out of the store and drove off in her car, leaving her stranded. It was not clear who had actually canceled the wedding, but it was obvious to each of them that it was off.

In the previous chapter, we saw that communication operates on several levels concurrently. For example, a distinction was made between the surface content of a message and the underlying feelings which the sender is trying to convey. Techniques of creative listening were suggested to enable the listener to check out his understanding of the underlying feelings in the message.

However, cautioning listeners not to be critical in their responses, and senders not to attack in expressing themselves, introduces yet another element of communication. The *style* of a message is as crucial as its content. Messages expressed in a challenging, power-assertive, competitive mode are very different in their effects from messages given in a supportive, noncritical, noncompetitive manner. Indeed, style alone can convey a message about the relationship independently of the surface content or even of the underlying feelings.

Take the couple in the men's shop with whom we began. Whenever someone tries to tell another person what to do, and does it in a way that leads the person to perceive the advice as judgmental or critical, that's communication in the competitive mode. Similarly, when anyone counters such an apparently preemptive definition of the relationship with resistance, denial or passivity, that too is competitive. The person who succeeds in such an exchange is said to be "one up" and the one who fails "one down"; in fact, however—as the couple in question demonstrate—everybody loses, since the relationship between them is invariably a casualty.

When I spoke to this couple later, they realized it was not sensible to let even such a painful and humiliating experience determine the whole course of their lives. Still, they did not know how to interpret the fracas in any reassuring way, and so presented themselves for counseling. As we analyzed the messages they exchanged—as we recast the wedding-suit incident in terms of the objective content of the communications involved, the actual motivation behind the communication by the sender and the motivation perceived by the receiver—it became clear to both of them that neither was stupid, or dictatorial, or even resistive, but rather, misperceiving. As a result, through a series of such counseling experiences, they developed a style of communication that was supportive and issue-centered rather than combative and misdirected.

Let me give you the analysis we worked out at the first session:

MAN'S MESSAGE #1

OBJECTIVE CONTENT OF COMMUNICATIVE BEHAVIOR	ACTUAL MOTIVATION FOR BEHAVIOR	MOTIVATION PERCEIVED BY THE OTHER PERSON
He walks to back of store to talk to salesman near loud suits.	It's been years since I bought a suit. I want to find out from the salesman if they can fit me and what suits cost these days before looking at any particular suits.	I don't care about your opinion, Beverly. The salesman and I will decide on a suit for our wedding; perhaps one of these nice colorful ones here.

WOMAN'S MESSAGE #1

OBJECTIVE CONTENT OF COMMUNICATIVE BEHAVIOR	ACTUAL MOTIVATION FOR BEHAVIOR	MOTIVATION PERCEIVED BY THE OTHER PERSON
"Henry, not one of those. The ones you want to look at are over here."	I want to be part of this decision. These are the appropriate suits for a wedding, not those garish ones you and the salesman are looking at.	Henry, you are an inexperienced clod and you know nothing compared with me. Come here immediately and I will show you what you must do.

MAN'S MESSAGE #2

He ignores her.	I am a grown man who does not need to be talked to like a four-year-old. I refuse to respond to such a public put-down.	I don't care about your feelings, Beverly, or about you. I will get one of these suits if I want to, whether you like it or not.

WOMAN'S MESSAGE #2

"Henry, what can you be thinking? You can't get married in one of those. Now come over here and look at one of these sensible ones."	I can't believe that you would ignore me and listen to that salesman. It's me you're marrying. Show me that you do love me and have a little good sense by coming here to look at something decent.	You are stupid Henry, stupid. If you don't hurry right over here and do as I say I won't marry you.

MAN'S MESSAGE #3

He ignores her again.	I will attempt to preserve my dignity even in the midst of this incredible humiliation.	I will buy this suit, Beverly, and nothing you say will stop me. You and your feelings mean nothing to me.

WOMAN'S MESSAGE #3

OBJECTIVE CONTENT OF COMMUNICATIVE BEHAVIOR	ACTUAL MOTIVATION FOR BEHAVIOR	MOTIVATION PERCEIVED BY THE OTHER PERSON
"Henry, will you listen to what I am telling you? I refuse to marry anybody dressed up like some vaudeville comedian!"	I am so hurt and angry, I can't see how I could marry someone who cares so little for me.	You have absolutely no sense at all. I am warning you, Henry, I will not marry anyone who doesn't do exactly as I say—instantly.

MAN'S MESSAGE #4

He walks out and drives off in her car, leaving her stranded.	I will not put up with this public humiliation any longer—and I will not marry you if that is how you feel.	Beverly, I despise you. I am deserting you. I want to publicly humiliate you.

It is clear that this scene could have been handled differently if one of two things had happened. First, if either of them had attempted to get at the partner's underlying feelings in the way described in the last chapter, the message the partner received would have been automatically changed from a competitive one to a more supportive one. The act of listening says, "I care; I want to know how you feel; you are important to me."

But second (since that would have required a calmness that was in short supply under the circumstances), one or the other could have identified and labeled the apparent put-down so that it could have been dealt with. Perhaps the first point in the exchange at which that might have been effective was after her initial comment. He might have walked over to her and said, "Bev, you make me feel like a child when you talk to me like that in public. I'm just talking to this fellow about costs and sizes. I'll come over in a minute."

Their second chance came when he simply ignored her. Admittedly, it is always more difficult to deal with such passively expressed hostility; nevertheless, she might have walked over to him and said, "Hey, I feel kind of left out. I hope you guys aren't going to decide on a wedding suit without the bride's getting a vote." There is an assertive complaint in that approach, to be sure, but the touch of humor in it gives it a style that is far less combative and threatening than it might have been, and leaves him the option of responding with banter rather than naked hostility.

Over a period of time, this couple worked out an agreement that when one of them was offended by an apparent put-down he would raise his hand. When that happened, the conversation was put on "hold" until the competitive issue had been settled; then they returned to the original content issue. On one occasion the bride confessed that she sat up in bed and turned on the light so that he could see her raised hand. Obviously, a more flexible system might be better, but it worked for them.

I am persuaded that if the issue of apparent put-downs is left unattended to, the more important business of the couple is likely never to get taken care of. Instead they will get stuck in unprofitable competitive bickering. Nevertheless, nothing is more common than for people to refuse to deal with this stylistic component of communication.

"You're making fun of me!" . . . "No, I'm not; why are you so sensitive?" . . . "Why are you ordering me around?" . . . "I'm not ordering you around; I'm just explaining what has to be done." . . .
"Nothing I do pleases you." . . . "You're imagining it."

I have tried to train myself always to pay attention to people who object to the way I say something. More often than not, there is at least some truth to the accusation that I am trying to one-up them, to put them down. I need to apologize and start over in a different key—that is to say, in a noncompetitive mode.

Once when I was in training at the University of Minnesota one of my fellow counselors was videotaping a session in which he was working with a husband and wife. Her style was to tax her spouse over and over with a long list of things he should do, things (as she pointed out) which any reasonable person would agree really should be done. His response was to do nothing except put on a hangdog look. On this occasion, as she was ticking off her list with particular animation, he said to her, "You know, when you do that you make me feel like a three-year-old." She was offended. "Why would you say a thing like that? I was being perfectly rational and logical and trying to talk with you as an adult." She started to review the objective content of the points she had been making. Happily, my friend had the presence of mind to ask her to watch a replay on the television monitor. As an added inspiration, he cut the sound so that all she saw was a woman wagging her finger. She was so taken aback that she blurted out, "I really do look as if I'm scolding a three-year-old."

MESSAGES IN THE SUPPORTIVE MODE

It has already been noted that creative listening sends messages in perhaps as supportive a style as possible. But there are other ways as well. The simple nondemanding touch, for example, is hard to beat. Admittedly, there are ways of touching that can convey competitive meanings: the sexually demanding touch, the nudge, the restraining touch, the condescending pat. But a straightforward, affectionately motivated touch can send a powerful positive message.

To some extent, of course, positives and negatives are in the eye of the beholder. In the last analysis, it is not how a message was intended that determines its effect but how it is received. It is therefore important for couples not only to learn what feels supportive to the other, but also to appreciate what feels like a put-down or an attack.

In a counseling situation, I often begin by asking the couple to list the things each does to the other that elicit favorable feelings on the part of the receiver. Then, as a means of increasing the ratio of positives to negatives in their relationship, I ask them to step up the frequency of their already established actions during the coming week. The results of this simple creation of "caring days" are often astounding even to the case-hardened marriage counselor. Increasing the positives may not solve all of a couple's problems, but it surely makes it seem worthwhile to work on them.

I remember one couple who came into counseling because of problems growing out of the man's former marriage. She felt that he was being manipulated by his former wife into being a free weekend baby-sitter for the children of his previous marriage, and in addition, she thought that the financial arrangement he had agreed to was extremely unfair to her. She felt that having to compete with the children for his time and affection was like having salt rubbed in an already open financial sore. On his part, he complained that she was resentful of the natural bond he felt toward his children and that she didn't even try to understand his position. In the first session, it seemed important to establish what the present marriage had going for it, so that it might be tuned up before we plunged into the difficult problem they had brought in. When asked what he did that made her feel good, she acknowledged that he was generally good about keeping the place up and that she especially appreciated the times when they worked together on projects in the yard or house. She also gave him points for being a good bed partner, sensitive to her needs and, as she put it, "sexy." He said how much he appreciated her interest and support in his problems at work (which involved a series of running battles with an incompetent and dishonest supervisor). He also said she was a good companion, fun to be with (in and out of bed) when she wasn't mad at him.

It surprised them that some of the tension began to drain away as soon as they began to focus on these positive aspects of their marriage. I therefore recommended that for the first week they concentrate simply on increasing the frequency of the good things they had mentioned. He was more than willing, but she said, "Look, I think it's great that we're good in bed together, but just making it sexually or otherwise doesn't do a thing for our real problems. It's just running away from them." I said, "Not if we think of it as preparation for a successful attack on the problem next week. This week I want you to live it up with each other, feed each other emotionally, increase the diet of good things so that you're ready for the hard work ahead."

Not only did they have an exceptionally good week, but by the time they came to the next session, each had been thinking of possible solutions to the problem that were fair to the other person.

This principle works as well with children and others as it does with marital partners. One therapist I know had difficulty with his five-year-old son, Joey. The boy was, in the therapist's view, spoiled by his mother's habit of doing everything for him. He would not permit his father even to pour his milk or tie his shoe or hold him on his lap. Moreover, he tended to ignore his father's directions and run crying to his mother when his father corrected him. In the therapist's mind, the whole situation was the mother's fault.

One day he was counseling a young single mother who was at her wit's end because her five-year-old daughter, Karen, was impossible to get along with. In his best professional manner, he recommended a heavy dose of positives. She, however, complained that her daughter gave her no opportunity—that the girl's every act was rebellious and spiteful. The therapist took up the challenge routinely: he began an eloquent lecture on how she could make opportunities to praise her daughter, to sympathize with her . . . He was, in fact, in mid-sentence when he suddenly choked on his words and admitted out loud that he was being a terrible hypocrite. He explained that he too had a child who constantly angered him, but that on his own part he hadn't done a single one of the things he was advising her to do. Indeed, he confessed, almost his whole interaction with the boy consisted of such phrases as:

> "Will you turn down that damn television set? I can't hear myself think!"
>
> "Let your mother alone; you just had a snack twenty minutes ago and you don't need another one."
>
> "How many times have I told you to quit bouncing on my bed? It's not a plaything!"
>
> "Joey! You're going to pull that railing right out of the wall. It was not made to swing on."
>
> "Watch out! You almost spilled your sister's milk."

So, being at heart a fair-minded man, he agreed with his client that if she would try to inject a heavy dose of positives into her relationship with her daughter, he would try to do the same with his son. When he got home, he went straight to work: he asked Joey if he wanted to hear a story. Joey didn't. Well, did he want to go with him to the store and maybe get an ice cream cone on the way back? Joey was busy playing and didn't feel like it. According to my friend, if it hadn't been for having to face that client the following week, that would have been the end of it. Snippy kid! As it was, however, the prospect of having to hear her tell of successful efforts while he conceded defeat was more than he could bear, so he persevered. Eventually he got Joey to agree to go with him to the automatic car wash and ride through the machine as it slapped and brushed and squirted at them from the other side of the windows. Joey feigned lack of interest, but his eyes sparkled. By the end of the week, Joey was sitting on his father's lap showing him pictures he had drawn and sharing his observations of the world. It was humiliating! To think that all that time it had not been the mother's spoiling or the boy's inherited defects, but his own behavior that had built the wall.

The story has a sequel. Two weeks later, on Valentine's Day, Joey gave his brother and sister one handmade valentine each, his mother nineteen valentines (which surprised no one) and his father twenty-two. To become a twenty-two-valentine father in two weeks is quite an achievement. But the final touch came some weeks afterward when Joey's older brother was attempting to organize the family in a game he had played at a neighbor's house. He said to the family, "Now, to start with, each of you must tell of a peak experience in your life." Joey said, "What's a peak experience?" His brother said, "That's one of the best things that ever happened to you in your whole life." Joey said, "Oh, that's when my daddy played with me." I have heard that father tell the story on several occasions, but I have never heard him tell it without a catch in his voice.

I call that approach the Joey Treatment. It rarely fails. The first client of one of my students was a young man who was going out of his mind because his father, in whose clothing store he worked, was such an ill-tempered man. He literally never opened his mouth except to criticize. Everyone hated him, and they had a terrible time keeping help. The young man, however, could not quit because he hoped to inherit the business in a few years. Meanwhile, he could hardly force himself to go to work in the morning. The student counselor prescribed the Joey Treatment:

YOUNG MAN   But I can't give him positives. He never does anything but complain and criticize.

COUNSELOR   Come on, he must do something right. He's succeeded in business all these years. Just ignore the bad stuff and focus on the good stuff. You can manage that for one week. Anybody as mean as your father must get very few positives in return. I'll bet he's starved for them.

YOUNG MAN   Well . . . I guess I could try it, but I don't know. . . . It's not going to be easy.

After five days the young man called the counselor and said, "I couldn't wait till our appointment to tell you. I've been doing what you said, and today my father put his hand on my shoulder and said, with emotion, 'Son, what would I do without you?' That is the first time in my life he ever touched me except in anger."

EXERCISES FOR IDENTIFYING MESSAGE STYLES

Before a couple can modify the style of the messages they exchange, it is necessary to label them in such a way that both the sender and the receiver can recognize the messages and their implications. The technique of creative listening is a useful tool in helping the present exercise to succeed— especially in cases in which the style of the message is a competitive one. But for the sake of ease, let's begin with the simpler task of identifying the noncompetitive, supportive communications that already occur in the relationship.

Identifying and Increasing Supportive Messages

Each partner should write down (in private and with no time pressure) at least three or four things his spouse does that make him feel good.

THE RULES FOR THE LIST:
1. Each item should refer to something the spouse *does*, not something the spouse *is*. For example, a wife might say, "I like it when you kiss me as if you really mean it," but

not "I love your blue eyes." A kiss can be thought of as a supportive message, but blue eyes cannot—even though they might be valued.

2. Each item should be specific rather than general. For example, a husband might say, "I liked it when you told me what you really thought about that movie we saw last Saturday—that was sharing"; not "I like the way you think about things."

3. Each item should be unqualified. Faint praise or double messages completely destroy the effectiveness of the exercise. Partners should avoid such phrases as; "I enjoy ———, but . . ." "I would enjoy ———, if only you didn't . . ." "If you weren't overweight, I'd appreciate . . ."

4. The items should not be trivial. Leave out such comments as "I like the way you lick your lips" or "I like your handwriting."

After preparing the lists, the partners should find time to read them to each other. Every effort should be made not to criticize the other's list but to try to learn from it what comes across as a positive to your partner.

Next, each should agree to send one or more of the supportive messages on the list more clearly and frequently, so that their total exchange is enriched with positives for the following week. Remember that this commitment is for one week only. Longer commitments may seem demanding, but anyone can keep a seven-day commitment.

Finally, and this is crucial, each one should monitor his own commitment, not his partner's. The reason for this is obvious: the message conveyed when one says to the other, "Why aren't you doing what you promised?" is competitive and moves the relationship in the wrong direction.

Occasionally, people are so angry at each other that they can't think of (or refuse to admit) the existence of anything their partners do that is likable. I would hope that somewhere in the chapters that follow they might gain a different perspective; but if nothing in this book turns out to be helpful in moving them out of that kind of power struggle, it might be that a few sessions with a skillful counselor are called for.

Identifying and Decreasing Competitive Messages

After the week of "caring days," many couples are ready to try the more difficult task of dealing with negative, competitive messages. There is no reason why the "caring days" should not be extended into the second week, so that the work on negative messages can take place in a generally positive atmosphere. When both have agreed to move into this stage, they commit themselves to abide by some additional rules for the following week:

1. *Whenever I feel put down by anything my partner says or does (or fails to say or do), I will let him know in a nonattacking way:*
   "I know you like to tease, but I'm getting very sensitive about the jokes you make about my figure. I know I'm not *Playboy* foldout material, but it makes me feel bad to be reminded of it all the time." Or "When you ignore my friends when they drop by, I'm afraid I take it personally."
2. *Whenever my partner communicates a feeling of having been put down by me, I will listen in a nondefensive way:*
   Instead of "Aw, come on, honey, you know I love you no matter how you look," try "I hadn't realized I did that so much. I can understand why it might get to you." Instead of "Look, they're your friends; don't expect me to drop everything I'm doing to entertain them," try "Okay. I'd like to talk to you when we get a chance about how often they drop in at awkward times and how we might encourage them to shift their visits to a schedule that fits better with the realities of our life. In the meantime, I'll try to be more civil."

When I finally understand my partner's feeling—to my partner's satisfaction, of course—I may wish to express what I intended by the message [in which case the sender–receiver roles are reversed]. Or I may simply acknowledge that the message was a competitive one and that I can see why the other person felt put down.

3. *Finally, I will try to avoid that sort of message in the future and strive to communicate my needs and opinions in a noncompetitive way.*

This is one of the most difficult assignments in the book.

No one would try to make a tulip grow by pulling on it, yet nothing is more common than to try to get people to change by yanking on them. Both plants and people respond better to a little nourishment.

4

NEGOTIATING A JOINT SCRIPT

When two actors go onstage, we take it for granted that they are both going to be working from the same script. No one would willingly pay to watch Hamlet tell Lady Macbeth to go to a nunnery. By the same token, when two people marry, they put down their five dollars in a similar hope. Unfortunately, however, the comparison too often ends there: the scripts from which couples play their marital scenes are sometimes disparate. The resulting scenes have, of course, a ludicrous side to them; but until the mismatching of scripts is recognized and rectified, the performances can be less than fun for the people involved.

DIFFERING EXPECTATIONS

We all come to marriage with already formed ideas of what it means to be a husband or wife, of what is involved in living with other people. Often, our scripts are based on the marriages of our parents. This may be true even when the parental marriage style is consciously rejected in favor of a different kind of relationship. We may indeed achieve much of what we aim for; yet the parental model has a habit of sneaking up in the most unexpected places.

I knew a young man who came from a family with five members and two bathrooms. In his house, there were strict rules on the subject of going to the bathroom. When the door was shut, no decent person would think of even knocking— let alone entering—since it was everyone's unshakable assumption that it was shut for a perfectly good reason. He confessed, in fact, that when he was a boy and it was his turn to do the dishes, he would sometimes take a book into the bathroom and read for a half hour or so. Meanwhile, his mother, who couldn't stand to see dirty dishes sit unattended, would do them. When he reappeared, he would say, "Gee, Mom, you should have left them; I was going to do them," and she would say, "Oh, it's all right. You can do them next time." What she did not even think of doing was inquire what kept him so long in the john.

By chance he married a girl who came from a similar educational, religious and racial background but who lived in a house with five people and one bathroom. It was the custom in that house to walk into and out of the bathroom at will, and it was not uncommon for two or three people to be using the various facilities at the same time.

The couple married, confident that their marital script had been truly discussed and agreed upon. But the first time she walked in on him in the bathroom, he was so taken aback that he would have disappeared into the plumbing had it been possible. He felt trapped and embarrassed, yet he couldn't discuss the matter. She could tell that something was wrong, but was confused as to what it might be. It took them months of tongue-tied trial and error before they finally worked out a joint script.

My own marriage provides another example. I would have sworn that my bride and I had discussed every aspect of life and love. We had known each other from kindergarten, dated from the tenth grade, were engaged for a year and a half. No one could have convinced me that there was reason for mismatched scripts.

But we never discussed what happens when you are sick. For that matter, if someone had suggested we discuss it, I would have laughed at him. Every right-thinking person knew what you should do when you get sick. You go to bed. That is your part. Then your mother, or whoever loves you, pumps you full of fruit juice. It doesn't matter what you are sick with, you get well in direct proportion to the volume of fruit juice you put through your system. If any unenlightened person had challenged the efficacy of this regimen, I could have explained that the fluid washed the poisons from your body and the vitamin C had universally recognized healing properties. Of course, you didn't use artificially sweetened juice: that turned the blood acid. And you didn't drink milk: that produced mucus. And clearly, solids were so inappropriate as to be out of the question altogether. It never occurred to me that a civilized person could deal with illness in any other fashion.

Oh, I had read of certain groups who thought the healing elixir was chicken soup instead of juice, but it was clear to me that unlimited quantities of unsweetened fruit juice were the True Revealed Treatment for all ills.

Well, I married this girl I had known all my life, and in the natural sequence of events, I caught the flu. Of course I knew what to do. I went to bed and waited. But nothing happened. Nothing. I couldn't believe it! Here I was sick, and the woman I loved was withholding the only possible restorative. I simply could not imagine any explanation that would fit. Couldn't she tell I was sick? We had an efficiency apartment; obviously, she could hardly have overlooked the fact that I was in bed in the middle of the day moaning and groaning and being dehydrated before her very eyes. Did she not love me? Apparently this was not the answer, since she seemed to be in a cheerful mood, singing as she worked. Besides, she really wasn't the type to take out her pique on a sick man. Nevertheless, it was true that I was sick and in bed, and that so far there had been absolutely no move to get me a single drop of anything.

I was so hurt, I would have left if I hadn't been feeling so bad. Instead, I decided to give her the benefit of the doubt. I said to her weakly, "Honey, I didn't realize there wasn't any juice in the house." She looked up from her sewing and said pleasantly, "Oh, I think we have some." Then, since I was too confused to respond, she volunteered, "You want me to get you some juice—is that it?" "Oh, no," I said, "I could probably manage it myself." "Don't be silly," she said, "You lie right there and I'll get it for you." And she did—a little four-ounce glass of juice. Period. As I learned later, the only time they ever drank juice at her house was on alternate Tuesdays when they would grace breakfast with a drop in a thimble-sized "juice glass." In my family, our "juice glasses" were 12-ounce and there was always someone standing by to refill them.

This went on for years, every time I got sick. At last, my wife said to me one day with tears in her eyes, "What is it with you and juice? I don't think I can stand to go through another illness with you. It's like a bad dream. You are constantly groaning and grousing about juice. But when I get it for you, it doesn't do any good. What is it you want?" So I tried to explain to her what juice meant to me when I was sick. Actually, I had never put the concept into words before, and the more clearly I explained it the sillier it sounded. It spoiled sickness for me for good. I have rarely missed a day of work since.

Let me give two other examples. One young engaged couple took my class on courtship and marriage and apparently grasped the concepts well. Their progress showed a good understanding of the principles of communication and emotional space, and I confidently agreed with their assessment that theirs would be an unusually rewarding and successful relationship. The week after graduation, they married. Six weeks later, however, I got a telephone call from the young woman. She said, between sobs, that they had not spoken to each other for the past four weeks . . . that it was over a stupid, stupid thing and they needed to come in and see me about it . . . but if I thought she was going to back down, I was wrong.

What had happened was this: As with many modern couples, both were employed and each had promised to take a share of the housework. She got home a couple of hours before he did, so they agreed that she would do the laundry and shopping and he would take care of the cooking. The night they got back from the honeymoon, he prepared for bed exactly as he had done all his life: he took off his shirt and dropped it on the floor, along with his socks and underwear. The next morning, he put on a clean shirt, socks and underwear and went to work. When he got home that evening, he was somewhat annoyed to discover that the laundry he had left on the bedroom floor had not been picked up. That had never happened when he was growing up. Even when his mother was sick she had somehow taken care of her responsibilities. Nevertheless, he said nothing; but that night when he prepared for bed, he gave his wife a pointed look as he dropped his shirt, socks and underclothes on the previous night's pile. He was a bit surprised to note that she gave him a hard look right back, and seemed unusually cool in bed.

When he came home the next day and found everything exactly as he had left it, he got quite upset and told her that he knew she had a lot to do, but he didn't appreciate having to step over the laundry for three days in a row. He did his job and he expected her to do hers. He was completely unprepared for her explosive reaction. She told him that she was nobody's personal body slave, that he was acting like a three-year-old, that he could damn well pick up his own things and wipe his own nose. He was offended at this entirely unexpected and (he felt) unprovoked attack. The only sense he could make of it was that somehow she felt it was demeaning for her to handle his personal things.

He told her that it seemed strange to him that she hadn't minded touching his apparently disgusting body when they made love, but if his underclothes were too vile for her to put her hands on she could pick them up with a stick. They hardly spoke that evening. When bedtime came, and he flung down another installment of shirt, socks and underwear, she jumped out of bed, taking her pillow with her, and slept on the couch. They had not slept together or spoken to each other after that for four weeks. He, when the supply of clean things ran out, had taken money out of their meager savings to buy new shirts, socks and underwear. The pile of laundry at the foot of the bed had grown to Himalayan proportions. Each felt stupid and juvenile, but neither would back down. To her, it was a matter of basic human dignity. An adult was supposed to pick up after himself; doing the laundry did not include collecting dirty clothes from wherever he happened to drop them.

They both wanted passionately to break out of this humiliating impasse, provided a way could be found to do it without losing face. A careful probing of their respective scripts revealed that neither would object to investing in a $5.95 clothes hamper to be placed at the foot of the bed. His script permitted him to drop his things into the hamper rather than on the floor and hers permitted her to see taking clothes out of the hamper as a legitimate part of doing the laundry. Having resolved the hard part, they were able to address the problems of what to do with about thirty sets of unwashed shirts, socks and underwear.

The point of the story, of course, is not that the issue may seem foolish to an outsider, or that it was so simply solved, but rather that a young couple of above-average intelligence and insight could still get derailed so easily by mismatched scripts.

Just recognizing the problem as a case of mismatched scripts is often a large step toward the solution of the problem. It never occurs to most of us that there is more than one way to view certain taken-for-granted issues. The simple act of labeling our way of looking at it as a "script" suggests at least the possibility of rewriting or editing. It also implies that the two different scripts probably grew out of diverse sets of experiences and that each has validity in its own setting. Such a view makes it possible to see a partner's apparently unfeeling or irrational behavior in a kinder and more accurate light.

Two of the most revealing things that can happen in couple counseling are to discover 1) that your spouse's behavior makes perfectly good sense when his or her script is understood, and 2) that your own script does not represent a universally shared viewpoint—that others with different backgrounds may completely misinterpret what you do and say simply because they don't know anything about your script.

Both aspects of this were vividly experienced by a couple who came to see one of our trainees after a humiliating public quarrel. They had never before experienced anything so upsetting, and they could hardly believe it had happened to them. This couple had recently finished four years of graduate school. For all that time, they had lived in a cheap furnished apartment with thin walls and an offensively squeaky bed. Now that they were out earning money, they discovered that in addition to about four times as much income, they had also acquired credit. They found a lovely new apartment and for a while their chief recreation became shopping for furniture. Their tastes were similar: living room and study were outfitted without a breath of disagreement.

Then one day, while shopping for their bedroom furniture, she fell in love with a Danish Modern suite that included twin beds. It was exquisitely designed and constructed—and it was on sale! She oohed and aahed and bounced to test the springs on one of the beds, but suddenly became aware that her husband was neither oohing nor aahing nor bouncing on the other one. He was, in fact, staring at her with a grim expression which seemed entirely unwarranted. She immediately went into a sales pitch on the set: how beautiful the finish was, how simple yet elegant the lines, how well constructed, how relatively inexpensive, considering what they would be getting. "And did you notice," she said archly, "these beds don't squeak?"

He was clearly unmoved.

"Frank, what's the matter? Don't you like this set?"

"Yeah, fine. If that's what you want, get it. I'll sleep on the couch till they arrive."

"What are you talking about?"

"Look, if that's how you feel, that's how you feel. I really don't want to discuss it in a department store."

"I really have no idea what you're so upset about. . . . If it's the twin beds, I'm sure you can navigate the three feet."

"You have a perfect right to your feelings. I just feel like a damn fool finding out in public that my wife doesn't like to sleep with me."

"Frank, you're being a perfect idiot about this. Twin beds have nothing to do with what you're talking about. My parents have had twin beds for years and they're the happiest couple I know."

"Saay . . . I'm glad you mentioned that. My whole life's ambition is to be just like your parents."

The fight took off from there. It covered in-laws, money, sex, personal hygiene and just about every other marital problem they had ever had. "Right there in the bedroom section of Gimbels," he said later—and she added, "Of all the stupid things to nearly wreck our marriage over . . . furniture."

From a vantage point outside the value systems that produced these mismatched scripts, the reader will have no difficulty diagnosing them. To her, twin beds were a symbol of comfort and social status. A double bed was something young couples put up with until they could afford better. To him, the double bed was a core symbol of marital unity and reciprocal affection. His mother had taken him aside on his wedding day and told him, "For your father and me, that grand old double bed has been the keystone of our happiness. We can never go to sleep angry because one or the other is sure to reach over and apologize with a touch." He took it to heart, and he had never been so hurt in his life as when he saw his wife publicly raving over the chance to get out of their mutual bed and into one of her own.

When I ask classes to guess how this situation was resolved, invariably someone suggests they probably got twin beds with a single headboard. Other students correctly anticipate that when the wife understood what twin beds meant to her husband, she too insisted on a double bed.

I like that story. It reminds me once again that a large part of problem-solving is seeing the other person's point of view. Often, with people of goodwill who are not locked into a pervasive power struggle, the correct diagnosis of the problem leads directly to the solution. This is especially true in cases such as this one in which the issue involves a core symbol for one partner, but something less central for the other.

CORE SYMBOLS

Richard Stuart, one of the most creative analysts of the marital state, has coined the term "core symbol" to refer to those issues which are so central to a person's script for marriage that the validity of the marital commitment itself is challenged if the symbol is violated. What constitutes a core symbol for one may mean almost nothing to another. It is not at all uncommon for one partner to do something which according to his own script is only a minor offense, and then be absolutely astounded at his partner's "overreaction." In the case of one couple I knew, whenever there was a major argument the young bride would pick up her things and go to her mother's house for a couple of days "to calm down." He hated it when she did this; but she reasoned that it was good to separate until tempers had cooled and they could discuss things calmly. One night, however, as their quarrel escalated and she prepared to leave, he told her:

"If you leave, I won't be here when you come back. I have had it with your going home to Mother. If you leave this time, that's it."

"I don't even want to talk to you when you're like this," she said. "After a couple of days' cooling off, maybe we can discuss our problems without threats."

"Ginny, I mean it. To me it's not marriage if you can't work out your own problems without running home to Mama. Unmarried people go home. Married people hang in there. If you go, I'll know which it is for us."

She could see that he meant it. For him, leaving violated a core symbol of marriage. For her, it was a sensible strategy for dealing with marital quarrels.

In another case, when the husband was really angry with his wife, he would take off his wedding ring and throw it on the floor before stamping out of the house. To him that was merely an expressive and harmless way to vent his anger. To her it was symbolically a divorce. She had wed him by putting that ring on his finger; his taking it off in anger represented the repudiation of those vows.

In still another case, a wife confessed that although her husband's passivity drove her crazy, her own behavior was often hostile; sometimes she reacted for reasons rooted in her background which her husband didn't even know about. She then related, in her husband's presence, a series of traumatic childhood experiences which were truly moving. She ended by saying, "So if I'm a bitch sometimes, that's why."

On the way home, her husband jokingly said to her, "Boy, was that session ever worth the money! When I came, I thought all our problems were my fault; but now I see it's just that I'm married to a bitchy wife."

She felt so hurt and betrayed that he had abused the sensitive material with which she had entrusted him that she agreed to return the next week only to tell both me and him off. As she said, "I don't need marriage counseling just to be called a bitch!" I was able to calm her somewhat by explaining to her husband the nature of core symbols—how what seemed to him a merely flip remark violated the basic trust that she felt was the core of the marital relationship. He seemed to understand and be genuinely sorry he had unintentionally hurt her. Nevertheless, during the week that followed, in a moment of love play he said to her, "Come here, you sexy little bitch." She almost hit the ceiling, and when I heard about it, I nearly did too. (It is instructive that he was more impressed by my reaction than by hers. He tended to discount her "tantrums," but counselors are paid to be understanding.) I told him that I would refuse to work with a man who held his wife in so little respect that he would continue to violate her confidences even after the significance of her feelings had been carefully explained to him. (Clearly, this matter touched on a core symbol or two of my own, or I probably would not have reacted so strongly myself.) Happily, the confrontation was productive and the relationship began to improve from then on.

MAJOR DISCREPANCIES IN LIFE SCRIPTS

Often enough, however, partners in marriage find that they have scripts which are not just subtly or surprisingly different, as in most of the examples above, but pervasively and jarringly different.

Sometimes the differences are revealed in the appearance

of the pair. I remember one couple who illustrated this richly. He was stocky, bullnecked and muscular. He looked like a football lineman, and in the high school where they had met, that was just what he had been. Moreover, he spoke little. When he did say something, it was likely to be blunt and to the point. He never raised his voice or seemed to get excited even when provoked. His expression might be described as stolid.

She, by contrast, was thin, angular and voluble. She had heavily rouged high cheekbones and wore pointed glasses. Her hair was teased, her clothes were frilly and on the occasion when I first saw her she was hysterical.

Her complaint was that after eleven years of marriage the romance was "dead, *dead*, DEAD!" He never spoke words of love to her, never took her out, never brought her flowers or other tokens of romantic affection. His lovemaking, "if you could call it that," was brief and neither tender nor imaginative. He was dull, selfish, rude and totally lacking in spirituality (a quality she felt was essential in a man). In fact, he constantly humiliated her by dozing in church despite the fact that they had a minister whose sermons, everyone agreed, could have gotten a response from a stone!

For about fifteen minutes she recited his deficiencies, but he never interrupted or changed his expression from one of resigned stoicism. When she seemed to have made her point, I turned to him and said, "Well, what's your side of it? I know there are two sides to every story." He said, "I guess I don't have to tell you, do I, Doc? She's nuttier than a fruitcake." I laughed, but he said, "No, I mean it. Her father died in the nuthouse, her mother has nervous breakdowns every summer for vacation, her brother is an alcoholic and her sister has been married four times. It runs in the family."

C.B.   But what about her feeling that you don't love her anymore—all that long list of complaints she has?

HUSBAND   Most of them are lies.

WIFE   What do you mean they're lies? When is the last time you told me you loved me?

HUSBAND   I'll bet I tell you I love you twenty times a week.

WIFE   Oh, yes. When I ask you, plead with you, 'Please let me know if there is one spark of love left between us,' you say, 'Of course I love you; would I stay with you if I didn't love you?' But when did you ever tell me you loved me if I didn't ask you first?

HUSBAND   There isn't time in between.

WIFE   And I suppose it's a lie that you never take me out.

HUSBAND   (*very quietly*) I have never refused to take you out—ever. No matter how tired I am from working ten or twelve hours in the shop, I have never refused to take you out.

WIFE   (*to counselor*) Oh, yes. If I threaten to commit hara-kiri, if I tell him that if I have to stay imprisoned within those dingy walls one more hour I'll go absolutely crazy, then he'll condescend to take me out. (*to him*) But when did you ever in our whole married life ask me to go out with you? (*bursting into tears*) His idea of a big evening is to fall asleep in front of the television set. He never reads, he never listens to good music, he even hates musical comedy and he's a damn lousy lover.

C.B.   (*to husband*) Is that true?

HUSBAND   She don't enjoy it anyway, so I get in and get out. Look, the fact is she's a mighty lucky woman, but she don't appreciate it. I bring home every cent I make at the shop. We have a nice house with good furniture. Not many women married to a workingman have as nice a place. I don't drink up what I make like her brother, or chase women like her dad did all his life . . . like half the men in this town do. I love my family. I'd do anything for them. I even go to her damned church with her . . . (WIFE: Did you hear that? That's what he thinks of the Lord's Church!) . . . on the only day I have to sleep in. She likes flowery words like her minister's good at, but words are cheap! Any damn gigolo can say pretty words. I show her with actions, with everything I do, but she don't appreciate any of it.

It is clear from the dialogue that this couple have scripts for marriage that include almost no common elements. She had a long list of things that a loving husband does, and hers didn't do any of them. He had a list of what a loving husband does, and he did all of them. According to her script, she was trapped in a loveless union. According to his script, she was one of the few women in their community who had a truly devoted husband.

Once I had diagnosed the problem as a case of mismatched scripts (rather than stupidity, neurosis or selfishness), it became possible to work toward a resolution. In this particular case, I explained that the trouble was that she didn't count any of the things on his list—almost as though it were a foreign currency she wouldn't accept in her store. But in addition, he wouldn't acknowledge any of the things on her list as being legitimate tokens of love either. We began, then, by negotiating a new joint script which included items from both lists. She agreed to acknowledge the importance to her of some of the contributions he made to the relationship, and he agreed to choose from her long list some things to do for her or with her. This was tricky, because she was quite ready to discredit any gesture on his part by saying, "You aren't doing it because you love me; you're doing it because the doctor made you." We managed to get around that by giving him quite a long list and insisting that he choose from it only things he really wanted to do, provided he found at least three per week. Both accepted this, and after only one week she came back with tears in her eyes and said, "I can't believe it. I think he really has loved me all this time."

I cannot pretend that that was the end of this couple's

problems; but it was a very good beginning and illustrates the potential for negotiating even disparate scripts where there is motivation to do so.

NEGOTIATING IMPROVED MARITAL SCRIPTS

The beginning of any work toward resolving differences in marital scripts is to make absolutely certain that each partner understands what the other really wants. Nothing is so frustrating as to try hard to please only to have one's efforts go unappreciated because they miss the mark. In previous chapters I've suggested a number of exercises calculated to improve communications about such matters. At this point, I want to introduce an exercise designed to reveal to each partner the things which might be done (or left undone) that would mean the most to the other.

Few of us can really evaluate our behavior except within the framework of our own marital script. Probably most of us are only dimly aware that there is any other way to view our behavior. We know what it means to us and we assume it means the same (or ought to) to others. In that frame of mind, we can continue for years doing things (or failing to do things) without realizing that they are hurtful to our partners. Often, however, small changes in our behavior—changes that actually cost us very little—can mean a great deal to our partner.

The first step in this exercise, therefore, is for each partner to make a behavioral "wish list"—a list of wished-for changes in his spouse's actions that would make the most difference to him. The second step is to negotiate exchanges from the two lists. For example: I agree to spend at least twenty minutes a day with the children this week (high on your list), if you agree to be more firm in enforcing the television rules we have both agreed to (high on my list).

Some couples may be offended at the idea of bargaining

in a marriage. They may feel that the mere listing of important behavioral wishes should be enough, since each partner is supposed to care about the other. If it works that way, fine. Experience has taught me, however, that in most cases, changes are more likely to be made if the couple go on to the negotiating step. This exercise is perhaps most successful when the couple are either playful and competitive (and can thus enjoy the exchange in a zestful way) or somewhat cautious and mistrustful (and so find some protection from exploitation in the carefully negotiated exchange).

Instructions for "Wish List" Exercise

1. Each partner should give thought to what changes in the other's behavior would make the greatest difference to him. These changes should then be converted into a series of specific goals which the spouse might actually accomplish in a seven-day period. For example, a wife may have felt for some time that the greatest thing her husband could do would be to find a job that had more civilized hours or that didn't call for so much travel. It's not likely that he could actually change his employment in one week, but it is entirely possible (should he agree to it) to send out résumés, follow up leads or seek interviews within the seven-day period.

2. Next, each should write down three or four of the most-desired changes in a "Wish List." To increase the chances for success, the items on the list should have the following qualities:

   a. Each wish should refer to something the spouse *does*, not something the spouse *is*. For example, "I wish you would cut down on between-meal snacks—*not* "I wish you weren't so fat."

   b. Each item should be specific and concrete rather than vague or general. For example, a wife might say, "I wish you would spend at least fifteen minutes a day talking with me without my having to compete with the news-paper or television—*not* "I wish you would talk with me sometimes"; or worse, "I wish we could communicate better."

   c. Each item should involve behavior that will be observable, so that there is never any question as to whether change has occurred or not. "I wish you wouldn't use that kind of language in my presence"—*not* "I wish you would quit swearing."

3. After finishing the list, review it to make sure that the items follow these rules. Also check to be sure that they are feasible within the next seven days (there is no sense in a wife's listing the wish that her husband would get home in time for dinner at least five days next week if she knows he is going on a three-day trip).

4. Then share your lists with each other. Be sure you understand every item on your spouse's list—to your spouse's satisfaction. At this point you haven't agreed to do anything, so you can afford to push for clarification without commenting on how reasonable, or even how feasible, each item seems to you.

5. When both are satisfied that they understand each other's list, either may open negotiations by making an offer. The partner may accept or reject the offer or make a counter-offer.

By way of illustration, I give you the wish lists of one particular couple, together with the dialogue that occurred as they negotiated certain key aspects of their marital scripts:

HIS WISH LIST	HER WISH LIST
I wish you'd take better care of the house.	I wish you'd spend more time with the family—at least three evenings a week and weekends.
I wish you'd quit yelling at Rosemarie (the three-year-old).	I wish you'd share your feelings more.

I wish you'd be more affectionate in bed.

When I'm not feeling well, I wish you'd help out without my having to ask you.

I wish you'd quit smoking.

I wish you'd pick up after yourself.

DIALOGUE:

WIFE   But Mike, I'm not feeling well. You know I never let the house go to pot when I'm not pregnant.

HUSBAND   The idea is to make a wish list. That's what I wish. You don't have to do any of it.

WIFE   All right, but if you could ever stay home and help me, I'd feel a whole lot more like doing it.

HUSBAND   So make me an offer I can't refuse.

WIFE   If you will stay home weekends—

HUSBAND   This is just for a week.

WIFE   If you will stay home this weekend and help me get caught up, I will promise to keep the place up for the rest of the week.

HUSBAND   No dishes left overnight in the sink? No clothes dropped all over the living room?

WIFE   I'll pick up after myself and Rosemarie, but half the stuff lying around is yours. I don't see why you can't pick that up yourself. . . . Wait, let me write this down. This seems like a fair exchange to me:

1. I will work with you this weekend to really get this place in shape, and
2. I will see to it that my things and Rosemarie's are picked up, and
3. I will do the dinner dishes before I go to bed (this does not mean I have to do any dishes you dirty after dinner) if you will:
1. Spend the weekend helping me.
2. Pick up your own things.
3. give me a hand in the evenings when I'm not feeling well.

HUSBAND   Okay. It's a deal. Now let's go on to the second item.

WIFE   Are you kidding? I'll be lucky if I get all that done this week.

HUSBAND   I'm doing three things on your list and you've only agreed to one on mine.

WIFE   But the things on your list are all huge. I think one is all I feel up to for this week.

HUSBAND   Okay, but let's start next week about smoking. I don't think it's healthy for the baby.

Some couples find it helps to negotiate penalties to protect a bargain. In the following week, for example, the couple above made a bargain that she would try to show their three-year-old more positives (using the Joey Treatment, Chapter Three) if he would support her efforts at discipline instead of taking the child's side. Rather than make it an all-or-nothing proposition, they agreed to a penalty if one of them forgot and slipped. He agreed that if he failed to support her, he had to clean the toilet (a job she said nauseated her when she was pregnant). She agreed that if she yelled at the little girl in his hearing, she had to bake him a pie (which she used to do at least once a week before she got pregnant).

Such penalties, obviously, must be agreed to by both sides and should be minor, even fun, concessions. They should be enough trouble to provide added motivation, but not so great a burden as to spoil an otherwise successful week. In a few families, even fines can be effective penalties.

Here's another example from a different couple:

HIS WISH LIST	HER WISH LIST
I wish you would quit criticizing everything I do.	I wish you would not ask me to lie for you.
I wish you would not take our troubles to your friend Margaret, and that you'd spend less time with her.	I wish you treated my work with as much respect as you want me to give yours.

I wish you were kinder to my parents.

I wish you would invite some of your friends to the house. We never entertain anymore. I wish you would not stay up and read in bed after I'm ready for sleep.

DIALOGUE:

HUSBAND   I really have only one wish: I wish you'd quit criticizing everything I do. The other two are just padding.

WIFE   Maybe if you'd do some of the things on my list I'd have less to criticize.

HUSBAND   If you could guarantee I wouldn't hear anything critical out of you for one whole week, I'd do your whole damned list.

WIFE   You'd show more respect for my job? I don't think you'd know how. (C.B.: Actually, that's too vague to be easy to comply with.)

HUSBAND   Try me.

WIFE   I don't feel good about that. I'll tell you what. I'll do your whole list if you'll do mine.

HUSBAND   Fine. Then you won't call Margaret this week.

WIFE   I'll only call her twice this week—when you're gone—and I promise not to discuss us—that is our marriage—at all. And I'll phone your mother, although it's not all my fault that she and I don't get along, as you very well know.

HUSBAND   Okay. And I won't ask you to cover for me. (Really, though, how often do I ask you to do that?)

WIFE   All the time.

HUSBAND   Bull! And I will respect the hell out of your job.

WIFE   I'm serious!

HUSBAND   *I'm* serious! And I will invite Ken and Edith over for cards. Let's see . . . and I will *not* stay up and read past your bedtime. And you will not criticize me at all, in any way, shape or form, for seven consecutive days. Deal?

WIFE Deal.
HUSBAND You'll never make it.

This couple did make it, though; and if they did, nearly anyone can. If you want to try it, the following form may be a useful guide.

An Optional Wish Form

HUSBAND'S WISH LIST
1. I wish you would ...

_____

2. I wish you would ...

_____

3. I wish you would ...

_____

4. I wish you would ...

_____

WIFE'S WISH LIST
1. I wish you would ...

_____

2. I wish you would ...

_____

3. I wish you would ...

_____

4. I wish you would ...

_____

Negotiated Agreement, Week of _____

HUSBAND AGREES TO: **WIFE AGREES TO:**

_____

Negotiated Penalties [optional]

IF HUSBAND SLIPS, HE AGREES TO: **IF WIFE SLIPS, SHE AGREES TO:**

_____

5

DIAGNOSING AND BREAKING OUT OF VICIOUS CIRCLES

In several earlier chapters, I've made passing references to vicious circles. They constitute a particularly taxing problem in many marriages. The classic vicious circle has three identifying features: 1) the harder each partner tries, the worse it gets; 2) each partner focuses on his own intentions rather than on the actual consequences of his behavior; 3) each partner has a dark fantasy of what would happen if he changed his behavior and broke out of the circle.

One couple I saw several years ago typified the pattern. He was self-employed in a competitive business that took up nearly all his time. Although he provided well for his family, his wife became increasingly concerned that their two young sons (ages eleven and nine) were growing up virtually without a father. She made a two-pronged attack. First, she took every opportunity to "try to get through to him," explaining how much the boys needed him, how much she needed him. Secondly, she developed a series of contingency plans designed to "get the best use out of him when he was home." That is, when he walked in the door, he was often presented with tickets to the ball game or the circus or the planetarium "for him and the boys." She noted, though, with mounting concern, that despite her efforts he seemed to spend less and less time at home. So she stepped up the program and finally, as part of her increasingly frantic efforts "to get through to him," dragged him in to see me. It took only a few moments to recognize a full-blown vicious circle.

The more she tried to get him to stay home and be involved with the boys, the less he was there. The less he stayed home, the more she contrived. In a private session, he admitted that he was appalled at how miserable his marriage was becoming. He could never relax at home, and although he told his wife that the business was going through a particularly demanding period, he confessed to me that some evenings he stayed at the office when he had nothing to do (his office was fitted out with a couch, television set and bar). In fact, the real reason he had agreed to come to see me was that he had about had it, and if something didn't change he wanted out of the marriage.

The dark fantasy in his case was that if he did come home more, it would just mean more PTA's, baseball games and nagging. (WIFE: I don't nag you; I'm just trying to get you to understand how important it is for the boys to have a father.) Her dark fantasy was that if she quit nagging him, he wouldn't come home at all. As she put it, "He's hardly ever home now, even with all the encouragement I give him."

Both of them, therefore, were afraid to change for fear things would get worse, and so each kept on doing the very things that were making the situation deteriorate. It was only with the greatest difficulty that I was able to get either of them to budge out of the pattern. I tackled her—alone—first.

Here is just a fragment of a conversation that went on for about fifteen minutes in the same vein:

C.B.   If I can get your husband to come home by six P.M. three nights a week, can I count on you to let him do anything he wants, even if it's just to watch television? Will you promise not even to make a suggestion as to the program?

WIFE   No! What good is he to the boys—or me either, for that matter—if he's just sitting there swilling down beer and watching T.V.?

C.B.   One thing at a time. Let's get him home first. We can try broadening his activities later. This is only a first step. If I can't count on you to cooperate, I don't see how either of us can hope to get your husband to.

WIFE   I want to be cooperative, but can't you see that the solution is to make him understand . . .?

Eventually, I got her to say she would trust me for a couple of weeks and see what happened. Then I had to tackle him.

C.B.   If I could guarantee that you would be left entirely alone to do anything you pleased, could you arrange to be home at least three nights a week?

HUSBAND   Hey, I'm in a tough business. There are things I really have to do every night this week. It's not like I was in a nine-to-five job where I let somebody else do the worrying.

C.B.   What would you do if a big deal popped up on the Coast this week and you needed to be there to put in a bid?

HUSBAND   I'd be there. That's the way I do business.

C.B.   So you can arrange your schedule if it's really important to you. Good. I think this may be important. I agree with you that the way things are going, your marriage is in real trouble. In my opinion, if you can shake free about three nights a week, there is a good chance of turning things around. Why not try it for a week or two? I've got your wife to agree to let you spend your nights home any way you want.

HUSBAND   Hey, she could no more quit nagging than quit breathing.

C.B.   Try it.

HUSBAND   One week. But if she starts in on me, that's it.

That agreement took some careful monitoring and nurturing, but within a few weeks the man was spontaneously broadening his activities to include his boys, although he enjoyed wrestling with them or throwing a ball around better than organized outings of any kind.

. Whatever the content of the vicious circle, the dynamics of it are basically the same. I remember an insurance salesman who brought in his "neurotically frigid" wife to be "fixed." His diagnosis was that his wife had been taught by her mother that all men were beasts who were interested only in sex, and that this had so turned her off that even his most enlightened and persistent efforts to turn her on failed. And he had tried everything. He had read every popular book on sex, and several quite scientific ones. He could discuss *The Sensuous Woman*, the *Kama Sutra* and Masters and Johnson with equal familiarity. He had put up sexually explicit posters in their bedroom; he had taken her to the best, and the worst, x-rated movies; and he had tried every technique known. Nothing worked. At best, he could expect sex about once a month "when she finally gets around to feeling guilty," and even then it was "nothing to write home about... she just lies there."

She, it became clear, had not come in to be "fixed." She had come in to expose her husband for the sex-obsessed animal that he was, to let somebody know what she had to put up with. She said, "He's after me all the time. He never walks into a room where I am without grabbing me. Doctor," she said, "when I hear his step on the front porch every sphincter in my body tightens."

Both agreed that it had not always been that way.

WIFE   For the first four years of our marriage it was beautiful. What he said about my mother was true. She did warn me about men. So I was careful in my dating. Doctor, the ironic thing is that one of the important reasons I married him was because he was such a gentleman before we were married. I remember congratulating myself that everyone wasn't the way my mother said—that there were a few fine, sensitive men and that I had found one. And you were that way too, at first. . . . (*Cries*)

C.B.   Then what happened?

WIFE   One night—it was August seventeenth—

HUSBAND   Can you believe this? She has the date memorized.

WIFE   I wish I could forget it. Anyway, he came home late that night stinking drunk and wanted to make love. I had never turned him down before, but he was so obnoxious, and I hate it when he gets like that, so I told him I didn't want to. He said he didn't care what I wanted and tried to force himself on me. There I was in my own bed fighting off a drunken rapist. It was the worst experience of my life. But then to cap it all, the next morning he came in to where I was sleeping in the baby's room, all tearful and hung over and apologetic. Said he couldn't believe he had been so crude. Would I ever forgive him? It wasn't him, it was the alcohol, and so on and so forth. I was beginning to feel that maybe I hadn't been entirely fair, and I was letting him hold me when he started to handle me sexually. I couldn't believe it! After all we had been through!

HUSBAND   Honey, I was just trying to see if you still loved me—can't you understand that?

WIFE   Well, it was then that it finally dawned on me

what a first-class fool I'd been all this time. I'd been taken in by his sales pitch, just like one of his customers. But the thing is, I had finally learned the truth underneath the sales pitch. It wasn't me he loved, it was sex. He didn't care if it was me or a hole in the mattress, just so he got his precious sex.

HUSBAND   How can you say that? That's a bunch of crap and you know it!

WIFE   Well, that's how you made me feel. That's how I still feel. All the pictures and the filth. What has that got to do with me?

HUSBAND   Everything! It's all for you.

Again, the diagnosis is clear. The harder he tries to turn her on, the more resistant she becomes; and the more resistant she becomes, the harder he tries to turn her on. When I saw them, this circle had been getting more and more vicious for almost eight years.

As is always true, of course, either one of them could have broken out of the circle by refusing to play his part in it; a simple unilateral refusal to give the programmed response would have made the whole thing collapse. In this situation, however, it was easier to arrange a coordinated mutual disengagement from the circle than to ask either of them to admit that it might have been so easily ended long ago.

Of course, each one saw half of the circle very clearly: the half for which the other was responsible. He saw that if she were "normal"—that is, sexually responsive—he would not have any need to indulge in his single-minded pursuit of seduction. She saw that if he were patient and gentle she could be as responsive as she had been before the circle began. Each viewed his own behavior as a perfectly reasonable response to a difficult situation, and the other's behavior as inexplicable and sick.

In this case, moreover, it was difficult to negotiate a new pattern. The dark fantasies of both were particularly compelling. In private sessions, each one almost walked out on me when I suggested that changes in his own behavior were crucial to the solution.

C.B.   Frankly, Mr. J., I think you ought to just cool it for a while.

HUSBAND   Cool it?

C.B.   Right. Leave her alone. Let her make the advances if she wants to.

HUSBAND   (*long silence*) Doc, I don't think you understand my wife. She's just like a business. It takes twenty calls to make one sale.

C.B.   I know that's the way to sell insurance. If you get into a slump, just get on the phone, stop people on the street, hustle until you start to sell again. But your wife simply isn't responding to that. It would pay you just to cool it—do nothing.

HUSBAND   (*angrily*) I'll tell you what I think. I think it's pretty cheap for you to sit there behind your prissy desk and tell me to cool it when you're probably getting it every night and I'm only getting it once a month!

C.B.   Mr. J., how long since you last had sex with your wife?

HUSBAND   Two weeks.

C.B.   Then you have nothing to lose for two weeks. Try it my way for two weeks and if you don't like the way it's going, do whatever you think will work better.

Next, I saw Mrs. J. alone. After attempting to establish some rapport and letting her know that I appreciated some of her feelings, I explained the nature of the vicious circle they seemed to be trapped in. Then . . .

C.B.   It seems to me, that if you wanted to, you could guarantee a break in this circle even if he did nothing to initiate a change.

WIFE   (*coolly*) I'm not sure I get your meaning.

C.B.   Well, if you became the sexual aggressor not only would it shock and please him, but it would certainly put an end to his constant efforts to seduce you.

WIFE   Is that your solution, then? Just hop right into bed? (*rising, as if to go*) I should have known that if we came to a male counselor, that would be his advice!

C.B.   (*firmly*) Mrs. J., please sit down. I have, with great difficulty, convinced your husband that he should cool it for the next two weeks and leave any sexual advances to you. If he does so . . .

WIFE   That'll be the day.

C.B.   . . . and you make no effort to initiate sexual activity during that period, then I must assume that you prefer it the way it is and deserve what you get.

I saw them again at the end of the first week. They both agreed that he had kept his end of the bargain but she had made no moves. "I will when I feel like it," she said. He said nothing, but looked at me with a grim smile.

The next week, however, she surprised both him and me by initiating sex three times. The couple seemed to be redis-covering all the reasons they had married each other in the first place. Areas that were not remotely related to sex began to open up. Unhappily, it would be intellectually dishonest to stop there and leave the impression that they lived happily ever after. The fourth week following the breaking of the circle, he came home drunk one night and said to her in slurred tones:

HUSBAND   Baby, I love you. You know that, don't you? Nobody else could ever mean as much to me as you. None of 'em. You're the top.

WIFE   None of who? What are you talking about?

HUSBAND   Nobody can touch you. You're sweet and gentle and loving. I love you.

WIFE   What other people are you talking about?

HUSBAND   Nobody. They're all sluts. You're the only one I love.

It turned out that he hadn't always been waiting the full four weeks between episodes of sexual intercourse over the years. She just exploded. She pulled out of counseling and a few months later divorced him. But none of that changes the dramatic positive transformation that occurred in their marriage as a result of their escaping the vicious circle they'd been in. In fact, few things in life are more amazing than the discovery that an enduring pattern of mutual hurts can be changed overnight when it is correctly diagnosed and dealt with.

In the case of the vicious circle, perhaps more than in any other situation I discuss in this book, the diagnosis is the largest part of the treatment. From the moment that one of the partners sees the whole circle clearly, it becomes a voluntary circle because it is within that person's power to break it unilaterally. Of course, he or she must deal with the dark fantasies; but usually he can handle this by experimenting for a week or two and noticing that the expected terrible consequences do not occur. I'll come back to that issue at the end of the chapter. Perhaps one more example from counseling experience would be useful before we turn to self-diagnosis and treatment.

A young couple had been married about five or six years. She had a long list of grievances against him, at the top of which was his getting her pregnant before they were married. Currently, she complained, he was interested only in his souped-up car and motorcycle, on which he spent almost all his spare hours. He had no time for her, or the children, or their home. In one incident, he had agreed to put up a new acoustical ceiling in the kitchen, but had left the job half done for six months. In another incident, he had taken everything out of the hall closet to install shelves and then had left the mess in the hallway for weeks. But worst of all, he was becoming increasingly impotent in bed. She felt humiliated and outraged that she was cast into the role of sexual supplicant, especially since he seemed to turn on to girlie magazines and even bra ads in the newspaper more than to her. One night after he had turned her down sexually she woke up and caught him masturbating in the bathroom. "Even the toilet turns you on more than me!" she raged. I must add that she was one of the most acidly critical women I've ever known. Almost everything she said to him was a put-down.

The first few sessions went badly from my point of view. On her part, they consisted mainly of long tirades about what an inadequate husband and father he was, interspersed with tears over her own inadequacies as a wife and mother. He said almost nothing, even when I addressed him directly.

C.B.   Well, Mr. S., what is your side of this?
HUSBAND   (*Silence, eyes on shoes.*)
WIFE   Well, don't just sit there like a lump of dough, answer the man! We're supposed to be here to get help!
HUSBAND   (*Silence.*)

Finally I said, "Is this how it feels to you, Mr. S.: you just don't feel like performing sexually at night when she's been a castrating wife all day?"

WIFE   (*interest perking up*) A what?
C.B.   (*cursing myself for introducing unnecessary psychological jargon*) What I mean to say is, if you criticize him all day, maybe that's—
WIFE   What was that word you used?
C.B.   Look, I don't want to get hung up on the word. The idea I'm trying to get across is—
WIFE   No, what was the word?

C.B.   (*Sigh*) Well . . . at the turn of the Century, in Vienna, there was this doctor named Freud who—

Wife   The word; I want to know the word!

C.B.   Okay, okay. The word was "castrating." It means—

Wife   (*slapping her leg and breaking out into convulsions of laughter*) I know what it means!

Husband   (*Struggles against laughter and finally gives in.*)

To me, "castration" was literally a psychological technicality. I knew, of course, what it referred to physically; but in my world, the only time the word was ever used was in the psychological context. She, however, had been raised on an Iowa hog farm where she had helped her father castrate pigs. To her the phrase "castrating wife" called up the outrageously, deliciously vivid image of emasculating her husband with the kitchen shears.

Between gasps, she let me know that she thought it was by far the best suggestion I had made. The session dissolved in tears of laughter. The payoff came later that week, when she opened up on her husband over something and he said to her, "Well, there you go again" and made the sign and sound of scissors cutting. Both of them doubled over in laughter. By the end of the week she had effectively stopped her habit of constant criticism.

As sometimes happens in long-established circles, however, his half of it continued out of sheer momentum for a period of time. At first they both had trouble understanding the concept of passive-aggressive behavior. They had grown up thinking that passive was the *opposite* of aggressive. Nevertheless, when it finally became clear that forgetting, postponing, neglecting or withholding could express anger just as effectively as hitting or criticizing, the effect was dramatic. She said, "You mean that when I tell him I need loving, and he tells me, 'Well, you can diddle me if you want to, but I don't know if it'll do any good,' he's really giving it to me?"

I said, "That's the way it looks to me." That week, when the situation arose, she suddenly sat bolt upright in bed and said to him, "There you go giving it to me again." He got in touch with his anger and had an erection.

Once again, that circle was not the whole extent of this couple's problems, and they had to work on others for some time; but the sequence of events I have just described was a turning point in their lives. As in the previous examples, the key to resolving the vicious circle was a correct diagnosis that enabled each partner to see his responsibility for his own half. Once that was done, and the circle was seen as voluntary, the rest was relatively simple. The following exercises, therefore, have as their primary focus the self-diagnosis of marital vicious circles.

Theoretically, the ideal procedure is to have the husband describe how his wife's behavior makes him react, the wife describe how her husband's behavior makes her react, and then to put the two together. In practice, however, this takes a remarkable degree of objectivity on both sides, and the potential for getting into a hassle over the facts of the case is great. After all, there wouldn't be a vicious circle unless each believed he was doing what he had to do in the circumstance. It's upsetting to have to learn that in your partner's view, you seem to be the one who is systematically sabotaging the marriage. Furthermore, this whole area is like nothing so much as an often-contested battleground: it's hard to avoid the land mines that have been buried over the years.

In practice, therefore, it will probably be best if partners do their analyses of the vicious circle separately. The following outline is designed to help you examine your own situation in the light of the three identifying features mentioned at the beginning of this chapter. Remember, however, that especially because you're working separately, each of you must make an extra effort to be as honest and discerning as possible about the other's perspective.

The first feature of the classic vicious circle is the fact that the harder each tries to deal with a problem, the worse it gets. Sit down therefore, and

1. Identify a problem between yourself and your spouse that meets that description.
2. Write out in detail what your spouse does (or fails to do) that makes the problem worse (or even *is* the problem from your point of view).
3. In equal detail, write out what you do (or fail to do) either as a direct response to your partner's behavior or as part of an effort to change it.

Now, to get at the second feature (each partner's tendency to focus on his own intentions rather than on the actual consequences of his behavior), ask yourself the following questions:

4. What, up till now, have you thought your spouse's reaction to your response in 3, above, *ought* to be? Or, alternatively, what have you *hoped* or *intended* it to be?
5. What, on the other hand, has been your spouse's actual reaction to your response?
6. How has that reaction made you feel?

Finally, to identify the "dark fantasy" feature of the circle, ask yourself

7. What are you afraid would happen if you did not respond in the way you described in 3, above? For example, if you usually knock yourself out to please your spouse, what do you fear would happen if you did not? On the other hand, if your usual response is critical and nonsupportive, what are you afraid would happen if you changed that?
8. Try now, as realistically as possible, to reassess the outcome of such possible changes in your behavior. Try to think of

any outcome that might be more positive than the dark fantasies you have been living with. Even if what you come up with seems unlikely to happen, write it down.

Now go back and repeat these eight steps, putting yourself in your partner's place and trying to imagine how the same issue looks through his eyes. This requires empathy, insight and objectivity, but do the best you can. (Afterward, you might check your results against the actual answers given in your spouse's own diagnosis and see how good you are at appreciating someone else's perspective.)

Last of all, on the basis of your own two sets of answers try to delineate the vicious circle. For instance, the three examples in this chapter might be diagrammed as follows:

No. 1. The more she "tried to get through to him" on the subject of staying home, $\longleftrightarrow$ the more he stayed away from home.

No. 2. The more he tried to turn her on sexually, $\longleftrightarrow$ the more she rejected him.

No. 3. The more she criticized him, $\longleftrightarrow$ the less he performed as she wished.

Once the circle is clearly perceived, the solution is clear. Since the pattern takes the form: the more he does x the more she does y the more he does x, either partner can break the circle simply by putting a "less" in the place of "more." This is one exercise which, while it works better if both cooperate, can be successful even if only one is motivated to try. Provided the diagnosis is correct, either partner can successfully break a vicious circle.

Perhaps a few qualifications are in order, however. On several occasions, when only one of the partners in a marriage was willing to come in, I have succeeded brilliantly in helping to terminate a vicious circle, only to have my client suddenly get angry at the realization that she had done all the work herself without any help from her spouse.

The most vivid example of this was a young woman I saw for six weeks early in my career. For the first two weeks, she just complained steadily about her husband: his financial irresponsibility, his probable infidelity, his social boorishness. The third week, I had her do the exercise outlined above. It gave her a new perspective on her own contribution to his behavior, and she began to change her approach to him. The results were dramatic. By the sixth week, every single complaint she had come in with had been turned around. I was, I confess, immodestly pleased with what we had accomplished in so short a time. In fact, I even thought of writing it up in a professional journal. Our final session was a short one.

WIFE   Dr. Broderick, I've decided I don't need to come anymore.

C.B.   I fully agree. You've accomplished miracles, and you've done it yourself.

WIFE   That's why I'm not coming back. I'm divorcing him.

C.B.   Divorcing him! Why? I thought he had changed in virtually every area of importance to you.

WIFE   Oh, he changed, all right. But only because I changed. It just hit me this week that I've done the whole thing. He didn't lift his little finger. Well, I say the hell with him. (*Exit.*)

C.B.   (*Drops partly finished manuscript into trash.*)

A second potential hazard is that the partner who elects single-handedly to reverse a vicious circle may do so with such a flourish of trumpets that the other partner is moved to defeat the effort out of competitiveness or spite. Circle-breaking campaigns are best undertaken quietly and without much posturing.

In cases in which both partners are committed to work on the problem, we have noted that the diagnosis suggests the solution directly. Sometimes it is helpful to draw up a contract of the sort outlined at the end of Chapter Four. This would specify exactly what the responsibility of each was in undoing the circle. Such negotiation in advance helps preclude subsequent feelings that one or the other carried an unfair part of the load.

When for any reason the circle resists efforts to break out of it, it is sometimes useful to seek additional help from a counselor. (See Chapter Thirteen on selecting an effective counselor.) But however you do it, few accomplishments are more rewarding than breaking out of a vicious circle. All the energy that was tied up in escalating hurt and frustration and resentment is freed for more satisfying uses—such as getting a mutual-support circle going.

6

DEALING WITH RESENTMENT

TYPES OF RESENTMENT HOARDERS

Perhaps no human trait is more destructive than the hoarding of resentments. I have touched on this as one of the elements in the escalating spirals of hostility portrayed in earlier chapters. In this chapter, I want to examine more closely the pattern of resentment-hoarding itself: why people do it, what they get out of it and how they can give it up.

Since there are different personal styles of storing up resentment, it may be easier for you to identify your own if I present some of the most common varieties encountered in the practice of marriage counseling. Allow me a little veterinary whimsy, though: I am going to tell you about Hedgehogs and Foxes, about Magpies and Moles, about Bears and Hound Dogs.

There is, of course, a risk involved in presenting such a series of sketches. Almost invariably, people recognize their spouses more quickly than themselves. It is a great temptation to say, "Aha! I am married to a Fox. No wonder we have problems. Foxes are notoriously difficult to get along with. It says so right in the book, and believe me, the description fits perfectly."

Clearly, to tag your spouse with these new labels is no more constructive than tagging him with the old ones: "mean," "sick," "selfish," "lazy." As I explained earlier, this kind of labeling is merely a stratagem for either avoiding communication or shirking responsibility for your own part in a vicious circle.

The value, if any, of such a list is to give you additional images with which to reflect upon your own defective patterns of interaction. The first requisite for change is always a fresh view of the situation. In the second part of the chapter, however, I shall make a number of suggestions as to what can actually be done about resentment and its associated feelings.

THE HEDGEHOG. This breed of resentment-hoarder is found frequently among wives who show up for marriage counseling. There are male hedgehogs too, but the female variety is definitely more common. I have chosen the name because of certain similarities between the dilemma of such a wife and the problem of a hedgehog in cold weather. This small, spiny cousin of the porcupine is said to huddle with its fellows for warmth in the winter like other animals, only to find that the huddling is painful because of the quills. So it moves away until it gets too cold and then snuggles back until it feels pain again—and so on, back and forth, through the long winter night. Analogously, the human hedgehog has not only a prickly habit of treasuring resentments, but also a deep need for closeness and support. Presumably, if she didn't have such a need, she could just settle for a lack of intimacy in her life. On the other hand, if she hadn't learned to store resentments, her desire for support might lead her to settle for a passive-dependent relationship with her husband. It's the combination of the two that drives her (and often him) to the counselor's office. Ignoring for the moment, however, her husband's possible contribution to the problem, you can see that she is in a major dilemma even within the confines of her own personality system.

She is likely to have a history that makes her conflicting pattern understandable. Her experiences with love, even as a child, have usually been disappointing. She began early to feel resentment toward her parents (or other important persons in her life) because she was neglected, dominated or used in some way that she felt was unfair. In similar circumstances, some youngsters are simply cowed, and their self-esteem suffers accordingly. The hedgehog, however, is endowed with grit and responds with resentment. This is a spunky thing to do, and admittedly, it has survival value in an unsupportive emotional environment. It leads you to fight back, or to withdraw into a protected inner self; but in either case it is a strong refusal to accept the message that you are an unworthy person. It may even serve you well when you strive for success in some of life's endeavors. But since the secret of this strength is the accumulation of protective resentments and mistrust, it is subversive of intimacy. Closeness requires openness, warmth and trust.

The Hedgehog seeks closeness, yet out of her past experience she is constantly on the alert for fresh signs of hurtful or manipulative moves by her partner. At the same time, her accumulation of earlier pains and disappointments has made it difficult for her to give freely and fully to him. All too soon, like her namesake, she hurts or is hurt and so withdraws, having added not only to her resentment and mistrust, but also to her need for closeness. In some cases this alternation between "trying to make it" and "blowing up" occurs within the confines of her marriage; in others it propels her to seek different experiences with other men. But either way, she is more than likely to become cynical and desperately discouraged with her life.

The most powerful remedy for this type of vicious circle is the approach outlined in the previous chapter. Each partner assumes responsibility for his own contribution to the problem. The husband learns not to feed his wife's resentments and feelings of deprivation; she learns not to dump on him in ways he can't handle. Even without this cooperative approach, however, it is possible for a self-diagnosed Hedgehog to address her problem constructively. Some form of assertiveness training may be especially suitable.

There are exercises at the end of this chapter designed to help you pursue this goal on your own; many people, however, find that working with others is the most effective way to learn new patterns of response. The idea, in any case, is to deal with feelings of resentment by distinguishing between the strong, self-assertive aspects of your behavior that you want to keep and the attacking, hostile or competitive aspects that just cause you trouble. At the same time, you should also try to become less dependent: deliberately take care of your own concerns and learn more effective ways of evoking warmth from your mate.

Although this section has been addressed to the female Hedgehog, the male of the species will find the approach equally helpful.

THE FOX. The Fox, whether in the woods or in marriage, can be a villain or a hero, depending on your point of view. Like other resentment-hoarders, he is likely to come from a family that he felt gave him little or no emotional support. He found himself unable to meet the expectations of his parents, but he became very good at doing what he wanted to do while keeping up at least an appearance of conformity to their wishes. He came to view life as a game in which, if you don't look out for yourself, no one else will. As a result, he developed an uncanny ability to survive even in dangerous and hostile circumstances.

From his own perspective, most of the upsetting things

the Fox does are done without malice: he simply deals with immediate situations. Indeed, he may take considerable satisfaction in his ability to think fast and talk his way out of a tough spot. He finds that despite the risks, such tactics often bring him success. People are likely to admire his style and to find him attractive and charming.

For his wife, however, the charm eventually wears off under the rub of repeated violations of trust. She gets tired of being soft-soaped, tired of being disappointed, tired of his lying, drinking, gambling or womanizing. But when she confronts him with these things, he is invariably ready with a response. He may offer a pious denial, a man-of-the-world sigh for her idealistic naiveté, a detailed explanation of the exonerating circumstances of his apparent misbehavior or even an abject confession followed by professions of unworthiness or renewed assurances that everything will be different in the future. If his wife seems unmoved by these performances, it is probably because she has a season ticket.

However, since the Fox is usually successful in his manipulation of life, it is easy for him and others to overlook the fact that, besides harboring resentment, he may also be covering up feelings of fear and isolation. It takes a crisis of uncommon dimensions to put him in touch with such feelings. Perhaps the trigger is a drunken-driving accident in which someone is seriously hurt or killed. Perhaps it is his wife's decision that from now on, there will be no "one more times." Whatever it is, the Fox finally reaches a point at which he stops dealing with his pain by throwing himself into circumstances he hopes will take his mind off it. For reasons that are complex and unique to the individual, this crisis triggers a new response: a yearning for some more effective way of relating to the people who are important to him.

In some cases, he finds that by the time he is ready to reform, his spouse has simply had it and no reconciliation is possible. In others he may be able to convince her that this time it really is different. In either case, rebuilding a trusting, reciprocal relationship is not easy. Nevertheless, many couples succeed. The principles outlined in all the previous chapters can be useful in individual cases, although there is the risk that the gamelike quality of some exercises will tempt the Fox back into his old tricks of trying to beat the system. A good Fox can fake or subvert any exercise if he makes up his mind not to change his ways. Perhaps the most useful material from earlier chapters is that on emotional space. If each partner can keep from putting the other in a corner, the temptation to resort to Foxy escapes can be minimized.

The exercises at the end of the chapter on learning to be assertive may be of more use to the Fox's spouse than to him. After all, he has never been backward about expressing his needs directly. If his spouse can learn to be more forthright, she may be able to avoid simply responding to his behavior as a nag or as a wishy-washy martyr. I have seen many a Fox and wife (and a fair number of female Foxes and husbands) work through to a rewarding relationship.

THE MAGPIE. My visual image of a Magpie is a person chattering and pecking at a resistant spouse trying to get him (or her) to do something. Her resentment is rooted in a long list of grievances which are well documented and often reviewed. There is a sense of moral rectitude about the Magpie which makes her (or sometimes him) slow to see the need for change. From her own point of view, she has gone far, far beyond the call of duty in trying to make things work out. She is frustrated and disgusted at the continuing lack of real cooperation from her spouse—and she lets him know it. We have already run into a few Magpies in earlier chapters.

From their spouses' worm's-eye point of view, they seem to be common nags. From an objective point of view, though, they are unhappy women (or men) who have been taught by experience that if anything good is ever going to happen, they themselves are going to have to bring it off. Some among them feel they have been forced into a hateful role by irresponsible or passive spouses. Others feel comfortable being in charge and are upset only by the incompetence of their subordinates. In either case, their behavior is governed by a well-developed scenario of what everyone must do—supported, of course, by dark fantasies of what would happen if they themselves ever stopped cawing complaints.

In my view, nearly all the previous chapters can be useful to a Magpie—as can the assertiveness exercises at the end of this chapter. In particular, however, the exercise called "Disengaging from Power Struggles" is designed for her. As psychologist Albert Ellis once put it, she (or her male counterpart) should be led to replace the thought "It's terrible, awful and unfair that I'm not getting the responses I *ought* to get" with "It's a real pain in the neck that I'm not getting the responses I *want*." Alternatively, she might well replace the thought "My husband *ought* to do this because it's right" with "If this is more important to me than to him, it's *my* responsibility to make it worth his while to do it."

Although Magpies are usually married to Moles, who are, at best, hard to motivate, I have seen dramatic changes in the behavior of the Magpie's spouse and children in response to a changed approach on her part.

THE MOLE. The natural companion of the Magpie is the Mole, the stubborn, resistant spouse who reacts to his mate's criticisms by digging deeper into his burrow of passivity. In the extreme case, his withdrawal is so complete that he virtually disappears from the marriage, leaving the role of spouse behind him like an empty tunnel. To a counselor, he may confess a list of grievances as long as his wife's; but he rarely expresses his feelings to her except through nonresponse. Moles are skilled at surviving in a hostile environment with the least possible expenditure of energy. Long ago they learned that it doesn't pay to fight City Hall. When the heat is on, their first choice is to remain silent and do nothing. If that isn't enough, they agree to anything. But whatever they do, they don't let you really get to them.

Some individuals are Moles in every sector of their lives, while others are respectable achievers in many situations, becoming Moles only in interaction with their wives. Their pattern is extremely difficult to change from the outside. No one is more stubborn or more impervious to threats, bribes, sermons or attacks.

What is necessary in dealing with a Mole, therefore, is to help him voice his own complaints and define his own goals. Sometimes, when he and his wife learn to identify his non-response as a clearly hostile move, he can see alternative ways of expressing his feelings. If he needs help in learning the skills of assertiveness, the exercises later in this chapter may be helpful. Certainly, it is best if his wife is supportive, rather than critical of his initial efforts to change. For this reason, a joint approach is the ideal one.

When counseling such couples, I find it helpful if I can get them to see their problem as a power struggle or vicious circle and then proceed from there. Occasionally I will ask the passive spouse to go home and come back with a program for relieving the couple's problems. Naturally, I risk his forgetting or refusing; but some Moles come up with excellent suggestions and thus begin a real partnership with their formerly abandoned wives.

THE BEAR. In the personality of the Bear, a horde of resentments is matched by a powerful, confronting, domineering style which tyrannizes and alienates his family. Generally, his own father was a Bear and he knows no other way of dealing with people. Because of his lack of social graces, he is likely to be surrounded by those who fear or dislike him. It is hard for them to realize that he may feel unappreciated and lonely. Frequently he sees himself doomed to deal with ungrateful or irresponsible people who may depend on him, but who begrudge him what he feels he has a right to demand of them.

Bears are not likely to have a high opinion of psychology, therapy or books on marriage, and only a badly wounded Bear would even think of reading this chapter. However, if he can recognize his pattern as one that alienates him from his family and fails to get him either the respect or the results he wants, he might profitably study the Principle of Emotional Space (Chapter One) and try the exercises designed to convert his aggressiveness to assertiveness in this chapter.

It will be a difficult and challenging task. His wife can be of tremendous help by being supportive. In fact, flooding him with positives (the Joey Treatment) would be the single approach most likely to succeed for her. She may also wish to study the assertiveness exercises herself. Bears need to learn how others feel and what others want and expect. Only if they can develop a more realistic view of their social environment can they learn to meet their own needs without resorting to intimidation.

Few things are more satisfying, though, than to see a Bear release the love in those around him by learning how to treat them with respect.

THE HOUND DOG. The Hound Dog's sad eyes and droopy ears project a negative image which misrepresents his underlying potential. This style is more evenly distributed between the sexes than the others we have sketched. For convenience' sake, however, I shall describe the slightly more common male of the species. Although a true resentment-hoarder, the Hound Dog is most noted for his self-defeating, negative attitudes. His assessment of his personal worth is extremely low. He may be unusually gifted and promising, but at the last possible moment he slinks away from every real opportunity to succeed. His response to these situations reveals both aspects of his character: his resentment toward the powers that be, and his distrust of his own value.

I remember one young man who was a talented advertising copywriter in a small town. At the urging of his wife and friends, he sent off a portfolio and a résumé to one of the big Madison Avenue agencies in New York. The agency was sufficiently impressed to send him an invitation to visit and bring more samples of his work. It even sent the plane ticket. But at the last minute he decided that his work wasn't really that good and he didn't go.

Another Hound Dog I knew was a brilliant young philosopher working for his Ph.D. at a major university. His department recommended him for a fellowship which would have supported his final year's work, paying for travel to some of the great scholarly centers of Europe. On receiving the news, he disappeared for six weeks to "get his head together" —abandoning, in the process, not only his class of thirty-five sophomore students in Logic I, but also his family. He didn't tell anyone (not even his wife) that he was going. He just didn't show up. His department head was so upset that he canceled the fellowship. His wife, left wondering whether he was dead or alive, had only his past history of similar flights to comfort her.

The Hound Dog himself rarely has an explanation for his behavior except that it doesn't matter, that he would have blown it anyway. His wife, who may herself be extremely upset over the incident, nevertheless feels forced to reassure and comfort him because he can't handle her direct expression of anger. As one such wife said: "Harold and I have had three children in the last five years, but I feel I have four kids to take care of, and Harold is the biggest baby of them all."

When asked why she stays with this frustrating and disappointing male, the spouse of a Hound Dog will likely answer, "Because he's got such potential. If he could just get it all together, he could be a fantastic person."

The combination of resentment and a negative self-image makes it hard for anyone to convince a Hound Dog that it is possible to change. Nevertheless, individual or group counseling is often effective, and if he could actually be persuaded to do them, the exercises in this chapter and others might also be of some help.

ALTERNATIVES TO HOARDING RESENTMENT

As I have sketched these six varieties of resentment-hoarders, it has become clear, I hope, that one reason for hoarding is the survival value that it provides. In looking for alternative ways of handling anger, therefore, a prime goal must be to keep the strength and toughness that have served so well without keeping the prickliness, resentment or insensitivity that is so destructive of relationships.

As a step toward this, I give you two exercises. The first, *Disengaging from Power Struggles*, is of particular use to Magpies. The second, *Learning Assertiveness*, is for all the varieties of resentment-hoarders, since it provides an alternative both to aggressive personal styles (Hedgehog, Magpie, Bear) and to passive, self-defeating approaches (Mole, Hound Dog). As I've previously noted, exercises of this sort are not likely to be effective with Foxes.

Exercise I: Disengaging from Power Struggles

As I have observed in earlier sections, almost nothing is more frustrating and productive of resentment than an elaborate, unilaterally developed script for yourself, your spouse, your children and your friends. It is frustrating because when you try to live by such a script, you are condemned to seeing yourself as a failure (since neither you nor your children ever measure up), and to feeling rejected, because your spouse and friends never come through. Moreover, you are likely to imagine that you are surrounded by lazy, selfish, unfeeling, stubborn, underachieving, low-quality people.

It is extremely difficult to get anyone into the frame of

mind to resign as Keeper of the List, for two reasons. One is that the list itself is usually a good list, a reasonable list, a list that any jury of impartial observers would agree contained only virtuous goals. The point, of course, is that it isn't the quality of the list that causes the trouble. It's whose list it is. It is the old business of feeling-messages and style-messages all over again: what you *intend* and what the others *read* are two different matters. The object of this exercise is to get you out of the business of monitoring everyone else's behavior and so free you from the unrewarding power struggles which result from that assignment.

The second reason for the difficulty of change is that this behavior, being a vicious circle, is supported by dark fantasies of what would happen if you actually resigned as list-keeper. The number one fantasy, of course, is that "Nothing will get done." Almost as common is "They'll never amount to anything."

The trick in getting past these fears is to try the new behavior for short spells. If the dark fantasies actually come to pass in a week or so, it's never too late to go back to the old way. On the other hand, you may discover that even though it all happened as you feared, it turned out to be not so bad after all, considering the resultant improvement in your relationships. In any case, here is the exercise:

1. Think of as many things as you can that your spouse or children *should do, ought to do* and *would do if they really cared* but *don't do* (or do only grudgingly because you are always after them). Write them down in a list. If you can't think of any such items, go on to the next exercise. If, on the other hand, the items come bubbling right out of you, proceed to Step 2.
2. From your list, choose three or four items that are especially troublesome right now. Place each one at the head of a sheet of blank paper.

These are the issues that you, considerably more than

your spouse, want to resolve (even though he, by rights, should be the one to see the need for resolution). Right now you are locked in a power struggle over each one, leading to more resentment and less satisfaction all around. In the next step, you'll consider, one by one, optional ways of dealing with these issues without provoking a power struggle. Place an A, B, C and D on each page of your paper at appropriate intervals.

3. Listed below are four alternatives to getting locked into a losing power struggle when you feel someone else ought to do something but won't. Depending on the nature of the issue, some of these options will work better than others; but for a start, write a sentence or paragraph indicating how each one might be applied in your case. Even if you feel like rejecting a particular approach out of hand, be sure to write something as positive as possible about it.

To help you consider these four options, let me indicate how each might work in three arbitrarily chosen cases.

Case 1: The wife can't get her husband to pay the bills in his business without continually nagging him about them. Dark fantasy: if she quits, he won't pay any bills; their business will fail.

Case 2: The husband can't get his wife to prepare attractive, balanced meals like those his mother used to fix. He leaves articles from the food page for her, pamphlets from the Home Economics Extension and his mother's telephone number—but nothing works. Dark fantasy: if he quits, he and his children will spend their lives undernourished, sick and perpetually annoyed.

Case 3: The parents want three-year-old Renée to go to bed at 8 P.M. She gets up again and again even when they spank her. If they lock her in, she cries at the top of her lungs for hours. Eventually, they give in or she gives up—but only hours later, after they are all exhausted. Dark fantasy: if they quit, she will a) never learn obedience; b) never get enough sleep and c) never leave them any time to themselves.

OPTION A: RESIGN THE CROWN.

PRINCIPLE: Swallow your pride and cut your losses by delegating to the other person full control and responsibility for his own life in this area. Let him reap his own harvest, whatever it is. In many cases he will rise to the occasion, but if he does not, resign yourself to suffer the consequences.

APPLICATIONS: *Case 1.* She will turn all the bills over to her husband, explaining that it's his business and she's tired of worrying about it. Then she will forget the whole thing and let the bill collectors remind him if necessary. It will relieve tension and redistribute worry in a wholesome way.

Case 2. He will refrain from saying one more word, or sending one more nonverbal message, about her cooking. He will eat what she serves and shut up. If necessary, he can take supplementary vitamins, or snacks at another time, without making a production of it. With no pressure from him, she will be likely to improve gradually; but even if she doesn't, she will reward him for his philosophical acceptance in other ways.

Case 3. The parents will make sure the child doesn't nap too long, but then they will let her stay up as late as she likes. They'll save energy, and she'll get sleepy sooner; but if worse comes to worst, they can always get a baby-sitter and take off.

OBSERVATION: In my experience, most people who are locked into power struggles will "turn away sorrowing" from this solution, even though it is the cheapest and often the most effective. Their dark fantasies are simply too dark and too real. At this point they nearly always say, "So what are the other three choices?"

OPTION B: DO IT YOURSELF.

PRINCIPLE: There is an old and true saying that "If you
want something done right, do it yourself." Accordingly, if you want something done, and if the person
you feel should do it doesn't want to, it makes sense
to do it yourself the way you'd like to have it done.
After all, who ever said someone should do something
he doesn't want to do just because you want him to
do it?

APPLICATIONS: *Case 1.* The wife will do the bills herself.
It takes less energy than getting him to do them. The
trick, of course, is to avoid saying to herself, "Why
should I have to do my work and his too, just because
he's too lazy to do it?" The right attitude is "Boy, am
I glad to be getting these done on time!"

Case 2. He will take over cooking some of the meals
himself—without playing the martyr or complaining
to his mother. He may even come to enjoy it; and if
he doesn't make it a put-down for her, she might like
it too. In any case, both will enjoy the more relaxed
atmosphere.

Case 3. This is difficult, since no one can sleep for
anyone else. In this case, option C or D may provide
another way of taking responsibility for the child's
health, education and welfare.

OBSERVATION: The virtue of this option, like the one
before it, is that it gets you out of a destructive power
struggle. You may be tempted to say, however: "I
don't see that it's fair for me to have to do it, and I
don't trust him to do it by himself, so I can't see
either A or B. What else have you got?"

OPTION C: MAKE AN OFFER HE CAN'T REFUSE.

PRINCIPLE: Too many interpret this, at first, as including
threats of what will happen if the partner doesn't
shape up. The real point, however, if you select this

approach, is to find out from your partner himself what he would really like and then offer that in order to sweeten him to do what you want him to do. After all, it's your want, not your spouse's, that is involved. Why shouldn't you take the responsibility for making it worth his while? This also takes it out of the power-struggle category and puts it into a nego- tiated fair-trade format similar to those discussed in Chapter Four.

APPLICATIONS: These will be unique to each case, depend- ing on what the partner wants. One battle-weary hus- band (Chapter Four) suggested his price when he said, "You've got four items on your wish list but I've only got one on mine. I'll do your whole list if you'll just *shut up* this week."

OBSERVATION: Someone always complains at this point that this is nothing more or less than bribery. Quite so. I could point out that bribes wouldn't be used so often in business and politics if they didn't work pretty well. From a less moralistic perspective, though, I would add that reinforcement is a fundamental element in all learning and that one of the most effective ways to teach is to make it rewarding for the learner to learn. The next option is an even better example of this.

OPTION D. JOIN WITH JOY.

PRINCIPLE: Often the most-resisted task can become pleas- ant if one's partner shares in it, especially if an atmos- phere of play or warmth can be established. This calls for imagination and goodwill, but it can be effective in putting an end to established power struggles.

APPLICATIONS: *Case 1.* She will make paying bills a joint project associated with playful affection and other refreshments.

Case 2. He will join her in the kitchen, perhaps

specializing in the kind of dishes she doesn't enjoy making, but in any case being sensitive to her kitchen etiquette. He will make it a positive, affectionate time. *Case 3.* They will make bedtime a richly textured, playful family ritual. They will invest time, imagination and affectionate attention in it. One of them may lie down with her for a few minutes if necessary.

OBSERVATION: When it can be achieved, this is the most satisfying alternative of all. When all is said and done, however, you may still find yourself saying, "I don't feel good about any of those options. What others are there?" Well, there is always the most inevitable alternative of all: going back to the old familiar power struggle. Maybe another look at A, B, C and D isn't such a bad idea.

4. Having written out your alternatives, however, choose at least one in each of the problem areas to work on during the coming week. If possible, discuss this project with an understanding friend who can help you with ideas. Then actually try, for one week, to operate differently in these areas. By the end of that time, you should have learned what works best, and even made a start on extending the principles involved to other areas of your life.

Exercise II: Learning Assertiveness

The purpose of this exercise is to achieve some of the same goals aimed at in earlier chapters on clear-channel communication or negotiating new scripts. You do not, however, require the cooperation of your partner. The object is for you to change your own behavior—to avoid aggressive or passive-aggressive moves which drive your partner out of emotional space and elicit only fighting and running responses.

Carefully review your marital relationship. Try to identify two kinds of situations: those in which you clearly demand what you want and, at the other extreme, those in which you simply fail to make your real wants known at all. If none occur to you, ask someone who knows you well to help you pinpoint a few. If you still can't come up with any, this exercise is not for you. But if you can identify this pattern (and especially if it took your friend to help you find it), proceed.

Plan during the coming week to let your spouse know how you feel and what you want in two or three areas. The requests must be simply stated, with no implied threats about what will happen if they are not complied with. Indeed, the most successful approach is to assume goodwill on the part of your spouse; that is, to assume for the purpose of this exercise that he is not lazy, stupid, resentful, mean or indifferent—that there will be a favorable response to your request. If at first the response is not what you hoped for, stick it out for a week. By the end of seven days, you will likely be getting positive results.

To illustrate, let me give you some examples of typical aggressive, passive-aggressive and assertive approaches in three areas.

SITUATION 1: Wife wants to watch special musical on television, instead of the usual football.

AGGRESSIVE: (to husband) "Why do we always have to watch that stupid, muscle-bound violence when there is something really worth seeing on the other channel? I ought to have some rights to that set."

PASSIVE-AGGRESSIVE: (to self) Same as above. (to husband) Cold shoulder.

ASSERTIVE: (to husband—before he gets settled in front of the set, preferably as soon as she is aware of conflicting programming) "I know you're looking forward to watching football tonight, but there's a special musical on that I'd like very much to watch. What do you say to its being my turn to watch this evening? In fact, maybe you'd like to watch it with me.

SITUATION 2: Husband wishes wife were a more active participant sexually.

AGGRESSIVE: (*to wife*) "I hope you don't think it's any fun for me when you just lie there like a board. I mean, if you can't get with it, you could at least have the courtesy to pretend you're enjoying it. I'd as soon make love to a mattress."

PASSIVE-AGGRESSIVE: (*to self*) Same as above. (*to wife*) Sighs, mopes, withdraws, says, "It's nothing," "Forget it," "It doesn't really matter."

ASSERTIVE: (*to wife*) "Darling, I think it would be more enjoyable and exciting for both of us if you took a more active role when we make love. When you caress me and do your part of the moving it really makes a difference to me."

SITUATION 3: The wife feels it is unfair for her husband to indulge his expensive hobbies when he claims they don't have enough money to fix up the house.

AGGRESSIVE: (*to husband*) "You don't care anything about me and the children. Just as long as you get to go skeet shooting, you wouldn't care if we lived in a pigsty."

PASSIVE-AGGRESSIVE: (*to self*) Same as above. (*to husband*) Doesn't remember to do the things that are important to him; is cold and unresponsive.

ASSERTIVE: (*to husband*) "I think we need new drapes in the living room, and our old washer is getting past repairing. It seems to me that the next money we get in ought to go toward them before anything else—even skeet shooting. What do you think?"

7

COPING WITH DEPRESSION

Deep depression is one of the most painful experiences anyone can have. Sleep is elusive, yet enthusiasm for getting up and facing the day is even harder to find. Nothing matters: work and recreation are equally unattractive. It is easy to hate oneself, to withdraw from others, to find life itself a burden. In fact, it is not uncommon to think a lot about dying. But if depression is terrible for the person experiencing it, it is no picnic for those around him either. Spouses, children, parents and friends are likely to feel guilty, annoyed, frustrated or frightened, depending on their dispositions. Since depression is extremely common, most people experience bouts of it at one time or another, either in themselves or in those they love. No book on making marriage more rewarding can afford to pass over it lightly.

To begin with, a depressed person should always see a

competent physician for a complete physical workup. Often depression is related to physical exhaustion, hormonal imbalance and other medical problems. Wisely administered medication can be extremely helpful, though it often takes three to four weeks to have a noticeable effect. In this chapter we shall consider the nonmedical aspects of the problem—what a spouse can do to help turn things around.

Many people who become depressed are able to identify the causes immediately. Others, however, can see no obvious basis for their feelings; for them, it is often helpful to go over all of the major events that have occurred near the time of its onset. Often, changes that they felt had pretty much been taken in stride, or even welcomed, may in fact have evoked deep feelings of disappointment and unhappiness. In general, though, depression can be traced to one of four basic causes—or sometimes to a combination of them:

1. Loss. Some losses are so intrusive that they are apparent to everyone. Your lover dies or moves away; a limb or organ has to be removed; a job, a home or a pregnancy is lost. Other losses, while less easy to pinpoint, are still strongly felt. You may mourn the passing of youth, of faith, of innocence, of love. In such cases it is the symbol of the loss which triggers the response.

The potential impact of symbols of loss is illustrated by the case of the wife of a successful business executive. It was he who actually phoned me for an appointment to see if anything could be done to help her. He described her as being in the grip of a deep depression which neither of them could understand. She literally didn't want to get out of bed and spent a lot of time crying for no apparent reason. I asked that they come in together, since it is my conviction that depression is best treated as a pair problem whenever possible. In the interview, she insisted that there was no reason for her feeling so down. When asked to review in detail the events that had occurred near the onset of her depression, she mentioned casually that it occurred about the time her younger son had received notice he was accepted at college. Of course, she added, he wouldn't actually leave for several months. It didn't take much skill to help her to admit the pain which this symbol of imminent loss brought her. Her husband worked long hours, and almost every evening he was involved in civic affairs. If her son were to leave her, she would be truly alone. The loss would actually be the culmination of a series of losses which had begun with her husband's increasing involvement in things that excluded her. Her daughter's marriage had been another blow. Now she found herself confronted with separation from her last remaining intimate, her son.

On a hunch, I turned to the husband and suggested that his frantic pace didn't sound like much fun either. This caught him off guard. His cheek began to twitch. As he fought tears, he confessed that he worked as hard as he did mostly to avoid having to think about growing old in an empty marriage. His depression was only a little below the surface. It was as if she had been bearing the symptoms of a despair which they both felt deeply, but which he, till then, had given himself no internal permission to express.

Perhaps the most difficult losses to acknowledge and bear are those which society tells you ought to be met with joy or at least with grace. Sending a child off to college or to marriage or to a job in a distant city is supposed to be an occasion for congratulation and satisfaction that all is going well with the family's life—that the parents have done a successful job of launching their child. To mourn such a "normal" and expectable loss may look to many like overpossessiveness or even "neuroticism." Yet the loss is real. No amount of pleasure at the young person's accomplishment changes the fact that a hole is left in the parents' lives.

This problem is not restricted to couples in the middle years, however. Young couples are often at a loss to explain how they could possibly be depressed after having achieved some especially important goal in their lives. Perhaps they have worked and struggled for years to finish school, or pass the bar exam, or save enough to buy a house. Theoretically, when success finally comes, they should feel overjoyed, depressionproof, on top of the world. Yet the very intensity of the period of anticipation ensures that this achievement marks the end of an era in their lives. A major life goal has been lost through being met. A time of almost unique concentration and joint involvement is past. The loss is real, and the depression, while hard to explain to anyone, is just as genuine.

The birth of a baby can have a similar effect. After a long and difficult pregnancy, the child is finally born and joyfully received. Why, then, do so many women experience postpartum depression when they should feel happy? Explanations frequently cite exhaustion, or changes in hormone levels. True enough, these may be important factors; but there is also the obvious fact that gaining a baby means losing a pregnancy. What relationship could be more intimate than that between a mother and her unborn child—and what more irretrievable when it ends?

This class of losses—those which are supposed to make everyone happy—are the hardest of all to deal with because the pain of the loss is compounded by guilt over feeling bad. Few friends or loved ones truly understand or offer support. Those who help most are the ones who have experienced the same loss themselves and who are enough in touch with their own feelings to talk about them. Spouses too can be helpful, provided they simply listen well at such times rather than try to explain that there is really no reason to feel so low.

The key to dealing with depression due to loss of any kind (whether socially approved or not) is to realize that it is normal, natural and inevitable to feel bad when something valuable is removed from one's life. Too often a "stiff upper lip" philosophy prevents people from venting their grief. An appropriate period of mourning after a loss ought to be considered a fundamental personal right. Grief should occasion neither guilt on the part of the mourner nor undue concern on the part of loved ones. Men especially are likely to cheat themselves of this, however, and as a result the natural process is frustrated and prolonged. Accordingly, it may happen that the mourning period fails to run its normal course and instead stretches into weeks or even months of immobilization. As in the case of prolonged labor in child-birth, help may be needed to bring the mourner back into normal engagement with life.

If you are a concerned spouse in cases like these, you may have to do more than merely listen well. You may have to be assertive and actively instigate your mate's rein-volvement with life. When dealing with depression due to loss, you must remember that something cannot be replaced with nothing. New sights, new sounds, new or renewed responsibilities and activities are required. Often others who have suffered similar loss—friends, neighbors, co-workers, pastors, doctors or counselors—can help further the reengage-ment. Since one of your spouse's symptoms is an inability to reach out, you may find that your first job is mobilizing these others and getting them to do the initial reaching. Indeed, this approach is called for in dealing with almost any de-pression, regardless of its origins.

2. POWERLESSNESS. Depression due to loss of power over your own life and destiny is perhaps only a special case of depression due to loss. It has some special features, however, that warrant separate treatment. For one thing, the loss may not be easy to pinpoint in time. Often, it is only after a pro-longed period of gradual erosion that you find yourself feeling trapped, helpless, without any impact on the course of your own life or on the events around you. Your dark fantasy is that no matter how hard you try to change things, no matter how extreme your behavior, everything will continue as be-fore. If you had a motto, it would be "What's the use?"

Something very like this sort of depression can be induced in animals. Experimental psychologists have shown that if a dog is strapped down on an electrified grid and given shocks, he will quickly discover that despite all his frantic efforts to escape, there is nothing he can do. Eventually he quits struggling and just cowers in his harness, whining and shuddering and defecating helplessly. If he is then taken out of the harness and placed in a pen in which half of the floor is electrified and the other half not, he will never discover the "safe" zone if placed initially in the "hot" zone. Believing escape to be impossible, he simply doesn't attempt it. By contrast, a normal dog, placed in the electrified half, leaps about until he discovers the safe zone and then stays there.

If you were to try to retrain the fatalistic dog, you would presumably drag or push him back and forth across the line between the "hot" and "safe" zones until he got the idea that his own efforts could effect relief from the pain. Similarly, persons who are steeped in fatalistic depression must be shown that they are not really powerless. They must be taught that their own behavior can make a difference in their own and others' lives. Like the dogs in the experiment, they are not eager pupils at first, and if often takes considerable pushing and pulling to get them to try new responses. If spouses or friends cannot get them to move, perhaps a behaviorally oriented counselor or therapist might help. But in any case, once they begin to experience the effectiveness of the new behavior, the depression dissipates and is replaced by a more realistic sense of control over their own destinies.

This kind of depression is illustrated by the case of a man who was once sent to me by a minister. It is significant that he was sent, because he would never have come by himself. He did not believe that counseling, or anything else, could help him. He was at the bottom of a protracted depression, and his list of complaints was long. Business was bad where he worked and he felt it was just a matter of time until he was laid off. (Others who knew his situation felt he exaggerated the danger he was in, but what bothered him most was that nothing he could do would affect the issue one way or the other. It all depended on economic forces beyond his understanding or control.) Moreover, he had become sexually impotent (a frequent side effect of depression) and felt that this was a burden to his wife. Yet he could do nothing about that either. His penis just didn't respond to any stimulation, and he had long since taken to avoiding situations in which the need for sexual performance might arise. He also felt that his children were unruly and unresponsive to discipline, that his wife was constantly irritable and in poor health and that, as a family, they never seemed to have enough money to meet their obligations.

He recited this litany of misery and confessed that he often thought of taking his own life, "except I'm too chicken to do even that."

In this case, I invited his wife to join us, and we worked at negotiating some limited, short-term behavioral exchanges between them. Gradually he began to show more zest for life as they both began to behave differently. Some of the new behavior also involved new approaches to child discipline, and as a result, the children got more reinforcement for good behavior, as well as less involvement in parental disagreements. The depression did not survive even three weeks of successful behavioral exchange. He proved to himself that at least some important things in his life were within his power to change for the better. Interestingly, he said he was as much impressed by his wife's changing of her habitual patterns as he was by his changing of his own. We underestimate the power spouses have to be models of effective self-determination to their fatalistic, depressed mates.

3. BOREDOM. A third possible root of depression is the feeling that you are locked into a treadmill of unvarying routine. There is not a single oasis of excitement or variety from horizon to arid horizon. Tomorrow and next week and next year will all be the same: the same scenery, the same cast, the same script. This kind of depression is frequently

looked on as the occupational hazard of homemakers, but it can occur in the lives of men and women in many different circumstances. Its problems are often multiplied by desperate efforts to break out of the frozen life-scape through affairs, drugs, alcohol or some other mechanism of escape.

In any case, the treatment is to urge an increase of excitement and variety, first in the marital relationship and then in life in general. Often, this requires the spouse to rethink his own overinvestment in business, or children, or television-watching. Planning new activities as a couple or as a family, brainstorming all kinds of impossible adventures before concluding that only a few of them are actually feasible, inviting in creative friends or relatives to help spark ideas—these are the things that are needed. Once again, though, it may have to be the spouse of the depressed mate who first leads out. At least initially, the depressed mate may feel too pessimistic to contribute any leadership to the project.

Even people who have poor health or serious limitations can broaden their horizons and find variety and challenge. Some of the most effective remedies for depression are activities that are service-oriented rather than recreation-oriented, at least for a start. The depressed person may feel in no mood for "fun," or may feel too guilty to enjoy it. This sour attitude may, in turn, trigger resentful reactions on the part of those who are trying to help him enlarge his world. But an effort at service of some sort may increase self-esteem at the same time as it introduces variety. As the self-image improves, recreational activities become more acceptable, and more useful as antidotes to depression.

4. RESENTMENT TURNED INWARD. Many of us have been brought up in a way that denied us permission to express or even to acknowledge our anger. Thus, when others disappoint us or treat us badly, we find it safer to blame ourselves and feel depressed than to blame them and risk rejection or condemnation.

Sigmund Freud, the great pioneer of modern therapy, was the first to notice that if a therapist can help a person to get in touch with the unacknowledged resentment behind a depression, the depression disappears. The difficulty, however, is that when it does, it is often replaced by very clearly focused and now open resentment toward the person who triggered the feelings. Obviously, from the point of view of the one now bearing the brunt of this newly resurrected anger, this may not be an altogether welcome development. Indeed, she may wish devoutly that her angry friend or relative would get back into his depression. In the long run, however, everyone profits from a more open revelation of each person's actual feelings, provided effective ways of resolving the attendant difficulties are constantly sought.

As with all the other varieties of depression, this kind may occur in either the husband or the wife. In the following case, for example, the roles could just as easily have been reversed.

An attractive young couple were referred to me by their physician with the complaint that the wife was not sexually responsive. There seemed to be no physical difficulties. Both agreed that the husband was a tender and patient lover; in fact, he was widely admired by those who knew him as a truly nice man. Neither could come up with a reason why she was so unresponsive sexually. Although it was evident from the first session that this lovely woman was depressed, I made the mistake of assuming her depression must be a reaction to her continued inability to respond sexually despite everything they had tried. So for several weeks I saw her alone, trying to figure out what in her background had made her "allergic" to sex. I couldn't find anything. She had been raised with a positive attitude toward her body; she had experienced no sexual traumas as a child or teen-ager; in her courtship and marriage, her husband had been unfailingly considerate and kind. There seemed to be no basis at all for her aversion to being approached sexually by her husband.

Virtually her only complaint against him was that, if anything, he was *too* nice, not only toward her, but toward everyone— especially his mother, who was in chronic ill health. He treated his mother as if she were an invalid queen, rushing ahead to open doors, driving the car up onto the lawn so that she wouldn't have so far to walk, getting cushions for her to sit on . . .

I began to perceive that this young woman's depression and unresponsiveness were related to resentment of her husband's "niceness," particularly toward his mother. But it took two further pieces of information before the whole pattern emerged.

First, there was a dream she reported in one of our private sessions. In the dream, she was chasing her sickly mother-in-law among the piers of a nearby marina. The old lady was surprisingly agile and gave her a run for her money. Soon an angry crowd, seeing that she intended harm to a helpless, nice old woman, began to run after the two of them. By the time she finally cornered her mother-in-law at the end of the pier, the weather had turned ugly; she pushed her over the edge, and the angry, churning waters swallowed her up. Then she turned her face to the crowd, drew a dagger that she had at her waist and, before anyone could stop her, tried to plunge the blade deep into her own chest. At first it wouldn't go in, but when it finally did, it felt, to her considerable surprise, pleasurable instead of painful. As she awoke, she remembered feeling relieved that her mother-in-law was being pulled out of the water by the crowd—chastened but unharmed.

In the type of short-term, problem-solving therapy that is my specialty, I don't usually get involved in dream analysis. But this dream could not be ignored. The woman herself (who had read some Freud) had little difficulty in identifying the meanings of the symbols. Her mother-in-law was a powerful symbol of the very thing she disliked most about her husband: his superniceness. The stormy sea was her own raging anger, and the dagger that had a hard time entering her body but then brought pleasure instead of pain was, of course, her husband's penis. In effect, her dream declared, "I will not permit myself to enjoy sex with you until I have expressed my anger toward you for your slavish and unmanly niceness."

In discussion of the dream, a further piece of information emerged which completed the picture. Her husband made love in the same way he did everything else in his life: "nicely." It drove her to distraction. At every step he would inquire how she felt; he was continually asking her permission to proceed, and checking to see if this or that move felt good to her. After a moment's reflection on his style of lovemaking, she said quietly, "You know, I would give a whole bucket of 'nice' for one thimble of 'go!'"

Do not conclude that after this diagnosis they both lived happily ever after. As her anger surfaced, her husband was offended. After all, he said, he had done nothing except try to show his love and concern for her. It seemed a little unfair to him to be blamed for trying his best to be a good husband as well as a good son. If he had known that this was what would come of the therapy, he might not have been so ready to spend his money.

It turned out that her anger was a great deal more threatening to him than her depression and nonresponse. On her side, it was not easy either. It was difficult for her to feel okay about resenting a life-style that was so sincerely motivated and so widely admired. No wonder she initially turned her resentment against herself in depression and paid him back only passively through her inability to respond to him sexually. But as unwelcome as the revelation of her underlying resentment was, it was a necessary step in the process of working out the problem they had.

Notice that this kind of depression, while it has many of the same systems as the others (feeling low, useless, not interested in anything), may require a different sort of treatment. Since it is based on resentment, it may have a strong passive-aggressive component like the one example just given. That is, the depression may actually serve to "pay back" the offending spouse by withholding responses (not necessarily sexual) that are important to him. It should be emphasized that this is not a conscious strategy, cleverly employed to "get" the partner. It is simply what happens when someone has a resentment, but denies himself internal permission to express or even to acknowledge the bad feelings. It should also be emphasized that getting in touch with bad feelings does not solve all the problems of the relationship. They must be dealt with in constructive ways, as I have suggested in earlier chapters.

8

YOUR SEX LIFE

I have encountered good marriages that retained their vitality despite an unsatisfactory sexual life and bad marriages that survived mostly because of a terrific physical relationship; but both are uncommon. For the most part, the quality of the marriage is reflected in the quality of the sexual relationship.

As in every other aspect of the relationship, when problems occur they can be traced to a variety of sources. Every principle touched on in previous chapters can be applied to this area. Sexual satisfaction can elude a couple because of mismanaged emotional space, poor communications, mismatched scripts, vicious circles, hoarded resentments or depression. When these issues are resolved, sexual problems may simply take care of themselves.

When they do not, it is probably because an individual's sexuality intersects with so many other heavily loaded issues. It is physical and interwoven with all the feelings and attitudes and images we carry toward our bodies and the bodies of our mates. It lies close to the heart of our sense of adequacy and feelings about right and wrong. Probably no other element in our lives is so intertwined with our deeply ingrained beliefs about what is sacred and what is shameful, what is private, what is outrageous, what is exciting. For that reason I approach the present chapter with some diffidence, realizing that assigning exercises with sexual content may offend some readers. They may feel that this approach robs sex of its spontaneity or of its spirituality or of its romantic component. Yet my experience is that many couples can profit from these assignments. They are adapted from the techniques that the most responsible and successful sex therapists use with their clients. Their strongest recommendation is that they very often work. Although they are designed for couples with a variety of problems, those without any particular difficulties may find that their sexual relationship will be toned up when they try some of them.

SHARING SEXUAL SCRIPTS

In an earlier chapter, it was noted that individuals come into marriage with scripts for marital interaction which may be quite dissimilar. Nowhere is this more likely to happen than in the sexual area. The scripts may be based on parental models, on friends' stories, on books read, on experience with previous partners—on any of a thousand things. As with other scripts, they are taken for granted and seldom spelled out clearly even in an individual's own mind. Nevertheless they do reveal themselves, sometimes through the sense of disappointment that comes when scripted events don't happen or, more usually, through a vague sense of discomfort that things are not going as they should in the realm of sexuality.

When a couple feel dissatisfied with this part of their relationship, it is often extremely helpful to share their sexual scripts with each other. Many couples find it difficult to do this because one or both may view sex as so sacred or so private or so shameful that it is very uncomfortable to discuss in any detail. Nevertheless, it is my experience that a sharing of sexual scripts can provide the awareness needed to solve many perplexing problems in this area. It is like turning on a light in a dark room so that one can see more clearly what without time pressures and then read them aloud to each the real obstacles to shared satisfaction might be.

The couple who elect to share their sexual scripts with each other begin by writing down what would be the most exciting and rewarding sexual experience they could imagine. In order to be helpful, of course, these scripts should be scrupulously honest and quite detailed accounts. They should describe the ideal setting, how the experience should be initiated, how each step should proceed and how it should end. For most couples it works best to write these in private without time pressures and then read them aloud to each other at a prearranged time.

It is understood, of course, that when they come together to share these scripts, they are to use good communication techniques (Chapter Two). It is important to try to understand your partner's script. It is also important not to be offended by it or overcritical of it, since such an attitude defeats the purpose of the experience. Sharing of scripts requires trust and goodwill. If major differences emerge, the alternatives they offer for joint script-building should be carefully explored.

Sometimes, however, even nonsupportive reactions can be grist for the marital mill. I remember one couple who came to me because their otherwise good marriage was marred by a sexual problem. Intercourse was painful to her; she found herself avoiding it whenever possible. Her vaginal opening, in effect, slammed shut when she was approached sexually. Her gynecologist had found no physical basis for the pain and said that she was just too tense. He advised her to relax, and prescribed a salve that would numb the vaginal orifice and so lessen the discomfort. She and her husband found this solution unsatisfactory and came to me to find out what lay at the root of her tension. When they told me their story, they also revealed that on those rare occasions when he did approach her sexually, his desire not to hurt her was so overwhelming that he often lost his erection before he could even attempt intercourse. Each felt like a failure, and both felt trapped in a vicious circle which threatened to sour their relationship.

In the course of working on the problem, I had them write out their sexual scripts. It was not easy, however, for her to accept the assignment. She had been reared in a way that left her with little internal permission to speak or even to think about her sexual feelings clearly. After about twenty minutes of my most professional persuasion, she finally came up with the following script:

> The greatest sexual experience I could imagine would begin with an elegant meal. I can imagine candlelight shining on the crystal. A single rose is in a vase on the table. Violins are playing in the background. Afterward we walk hand in hand in the moonlight and eventually climb marble stairs to an exquisite Louis XIV bedroom with a canopied bed. There we would undress each other, make love and have simultaneous orgasms.

By contrast, her husband needed little urging to commit his fantasy to paper. With evident relish, he filled page after page. His script involved being awakened from a deep and innocent sleep by a naked, sex-starved female who stimulated every part of his body with every part of her body in every imaginable way (and in some ways I, at least, had never imagined). Sensation built on sensation until at last she brought both of them to a mind-boggling, earth-shaking, life-threatening mutual climax.

He was obviously pleased with his script and wondered out loud if it might have commercial possibilities. Her reaction to this story, however, was explosive. Ignoring the agreement to accept each other's scripts without offense and to discuss differences with goodwill, she lit into him. Didn't he realize that that woman had to do every bit of the work— that he hadn't as much as lifted a finger from beginning to end? Did he think that ideal lovemaking was just lying there on his back and letting her do it all? As far as she was concerned, he must be the "laziest, most self-centered male from the creation forward!"

This attack did not seem to ruffle him at all. He just grinned and admitted that she might be right—in fact, that all of his sexual fantasies had that same quality. For example, he might have imagined himself strolling along the street on some innocuous errand and then being ambushed by a group of teen-aged nymphomaniacs who dragged him into an alley, stripped him naked and gang-raped him. In all of these fantasies, he played the role of the innocent bystander caught up in a whirlwind of female passion. He never felt any responsibility for what happened.

Since his further fantasies seemed to upset her even more, I intervened and asked him what he thought of *her* story. The question sobered him. "Do I have to tell the truth?" he asked. I nodded. "Well, frankly," he said, "after a four-hour buildup of wine and roses and violins and moonlight... who could follow an act like that? Not me! I mean, when the great moment arrives and the trumpet sounds and the spotlight goes on, I can't imagine anything I could do that wouldn't be an anticlimax."

As they each contemplated the messages of the two scripts, it became clear that at least part of their sexual problem was the result of mismatched expectations. In his script, the female did all the work and he took no responsibility or risk at all. In her script, the atmosphere did all the work and neither of them took any responsibility or risk. No wonder their sexual encounters were rare and unsatisfactory. They needed to negotiate a new joint script that involved more atmosphere for her and more risk-taking and initiative for both of them.

NONDEMAND PLEASURING

Once the need for developing joint sexual scripts is acknowledged, it still remains a challenging problem how best to apply all that has been learned in other chapters to the sexual arena. More than words is involved, and most of us have never developed a vocabulary for sound and sight and touch and smell and taste. We are uncertain how to communicate our own feelings and still less certain how to read our partner's feelings. What is needed is an approach that has the following qualities:

1. It shows respect for the couple, for their privacy and individuality.
2. It is flexible, providing training in problem-solving rather than canned solutions; rules for negotiating rather than predetermined sexual "menus."
3. It is symmetrical and complementary, providing each partner with an equal opportunity to express and realize his or her own needs.

Among all the attempts to develop an approach meeting these criteria, by far the most successful is William H. Masters' and Virginia E. Johnson's "nondemand pleasuring" technique. It is, perhaps, the most valuable tool in the sex therapists' kit and is an integral part of most programs of sex therapy. Yet there seems to be no reason why its benefits should be restricted to couples in therapy.

The program consists of a sequence of three separate steps. Each step usually requires a week or ten days to complete successfully. Accordingly, it would be foolish for a couple to begin such a project unless they were going to be together for at least four weeks. Over this period, they should be willing to commit themselves to a minimum of four one-hour sessions per week. Clearly, this is a project that calls for full commitment from both partners; it is not the sort of thing that works well with one enthusiast and one foot-dragger. Therefore, the first task of the couple contemplating this program is to negotiate a mutual involvement for the entire period and to plan their schedules to protect the required hours. Not that the exercise is such a chore. Most couples report that these hours are among the most enjoyable they have ever spent together.

STEP 1. *Nondemand, Nonsexual Pleasuring.*
RULE 1. *The couple must agree to abstain from sexual intercourse or any other form of sexual stimulation for the duration of this step (seven to ten days).* The purpose of this is to free the exercise from any connection with old scripts. It is especially important to free this pleasuring from any hint of demand for sexual performance. When new patterns of interaction are being developed, it is counterproductive to continue old patterns. Besides, abstinence is widely reputed to be good for character development.

If the temptation to have intercourse proves too great on some occasion during this period, the couple should begin Step 1 again from that point. If the problem keeps recurring, it probably indicates that this is not the right exercise for this couple at this time.

RULE 2. A warm, pleasant room, secure from interruption, is required. This may involve buying a lock for the bedroom door.

RULE 3. The two partners alternate being the Giver and the Receiver until each has had at least two and preferably three completely successful experiences in each role. Clothes are an encumbrance in either role.

RULE 4. The Giver:

A. Massages the Receiver's body front and back, from head to toe, excluding the genitals—and, if the Receiver is the wife, excluding the breasts as well. Often, a little prewarmed oil or lotion adds to the pleasure. It is not possible to do a good job in less than twenty minutes, and most people take up to an hour.

B. Takes his or her cues from the Receiver—who is fully in charge of the exercise. It is not always easy to set aside preconceived ideas of what the partner wants or should want. But it is crucial to let the Receiver set the pace and duration of the pleasuring and to follow cheerfully all directions given. Remember, the roles will be reversed in the next session.

RULE 5. The Receiver:

A. Focuses his or her whole attention on what feels good. The Receiver concentrates on whether strokes should be longer or shorter, firmer or lighter, circular, higher or a little to the left. For some this is easy, but for others who have never felt free to experience bodily pleasure for its own sake, it may be difficult to admit what feels good and to take responsibility for maximizing their own pleasure. It is crucial not to worry about the Giver's getting bored or tired. For one thing, giving pleasure to another is not boring. But even if it seems to be, don't fret. This is your turn: he gets his next time. Just relax and enjoy the role of Receiver.

B. *Communicates his or her wants to the Giver.* It is not enough to say, "It doesn't matter, just go ahead" or "Yeah, it's okay." This is, in part, a communication exercise, and while no one would want to have to keep up a continuous patter of instructions, there should never be any doubt in the Giver's mind about what the Receiver wants and how it's wanted. Much of this can be communicated without words. One of the most effective techniques is to guide the Giver's hand (especially over ticklish or sensitive areas). Sometimes it is helpful to demonstrate just what is wanted on one's partner's body.

Most couples enjoy this exercise. It brings them closer together, and after a session or two, most couples look forward to their next appointment with warm anticipation. It is a period of discovery. For example, while many may have discovered the joys of a good back rub, far fewer have ever experienced a thorough hand, foot or face massage.

Pleasuring and being pleased is always a sensuous experience; but at this level (Step 1) it is rarely an erotic experience. In fact, one of the precise purposes of the exercise is to separate physical pleasuring from sexual demands in order to develop it more fully in its own right. Since the couple may never have experienced anything like this before, it is not uncommon for one or the other to feel a bit awkward or tense at first. Usually this feeling drains away after a few minutes. If it does not, they should dedicate the first session simply to getting used to the exercise and not worry about completing the entire procedure. In this case, however, it should not be counted as a regular session.

If, after a couple of sessions, one or the other member

finds the experience tension-producing instead of tension-relieving, it is evident that it is not achieving its goal, and it should be discontinued. To persist in such circumstances would just cause or compound problems.

But assuming that the couple have had a successful and delightful experience with Step 1, they are ready to proceed to Step 2.

STEP 2. *Nondemand Sexual Pleasuring.*

RULE 1. *All the rules of Step 1 apply here except that the genitals of each, and the wife's breasts, are now included.* These areas are usually more sensitive than others, but there are also things about the pleasuring of them that have to be unlearned—especially things uncritically accepted from the old scripts. Everything learned in Step 1 will be of value. It may be especially important for the Receiver to guide the hand of the Giver in these sensitive areas.

RULE 2. *The goal of this exercise is pleasure, not orgasm.* This means that the stroking should be light, even flirtatious, rather than focused, rhythmic and driving. This requires a new outlook, since, in the past, stimulation of the genitals has almost always been associated with erotic arousal and tightly focused on the goal of orgasm. In this exercise, orgasm should be avoided, or at least postponed as long as possible. Soft, caressing strokes that do not concentrate on the genital area for extended periods are best. After a prolonged period of pleasuring, the Receiver may elect to guide the Giver toward a more focused mode of stimulation which ends in sexual climax. That is his or her privilege—but the worst possible violation of the exercise's goal would be for the Giver to aim at climax on his or her own initiative. That would simply be the old seductive script all over again.

STEP 3. *Nondemand Pleasuring Including Intercourse.*

RULE 1.   Using *everything they have learned in Steps 1 and 2, the couple should mutually employ their own version of nondemand sexual and general pleasuring. This should proceed for at least twenty or thirty minutes.*

RULE 2.   They should then proceed to intercourse, choosing a position that permits both to participate as equals. Once again, it is best to begin with a position different from the one the couple have habitually used. They may wish to consider the following possibilities:

A. For couples of whom the wife has usually been the more passive or inhibited partner: They should proceed to intercourse after a period of pleasuring in which she has been in full control as the Receiver. This is most easily achieved if the husband lies on his back while she sits astride him face to face. In this position she has full control of the rate, depth and rhythm of penetration. Since she is in charge, she can make sure it will be a good experience for her. She may wish to begin by simply containing her husband's penis—getting the feel of having him inside her in a nondemand situation. She may wish, in a leisurely and playful manner, to experiment with simply contracting and relaxing her vaginal muscles for a few moments and then perhaps experimenting with slow rotation or other movement that feels interesting and pleasurable to her. As she wishes, she may begin to thrust in a rhythm and style that pleases and stimulates her. After a couple of sessions like this she may wish to move on to a more mutual style such as one described in C.

B. For couples of whom the husband has been the

more passive or inhibited partner: At some point in the process of mutual pleasuring, the husband and wife assume the position as in A above and the wife places his penis in her vagina. (Even if it should be only partially erect, this can be achieved with patience and adequate lubrication.) The difference here is that this is a session in which the husband is the Receiver; his wife is to follow his instructions as to motions, rhythm, etc. As in A above, however, it is equally important to be experimental and leisurely. After a couple of sessions like this he may wish to move on to a more mutual style such as the following:

C. For all couples: Perhaps the most effective and flexible position for a couple moving from non-demand pleasuring to sexual intercourse is lying side by side, facing each other with legs intertwined; that is, she lies on his thigh and his other leg is between hers. This position permits each partner considerable freedom of movement. In order to make the transition most effective, they should begin in a leisurely and exploratory manner, in the general spirit of the earlier exercises. (After the two or three preceding weeks of abstinence, the rest generally takes care of itself.)

D. For all couples: they may assume any other position that is pleasurable to both, provided, once again, they proceed in a leisurely and experimental manner.

In any case, if they are to enjoy the greatest success, it is obvious that the principles of mutuality, communication, consideration and relaxed pace must be carried over into their sexual intercourse. After about a week of paying careful attention to these principles, the couple should be able to proceed to elaborate and incorporate them into their regular sex life at their own pace. It is the common experience that after this exercise has been successfully completed, sex and affection are permanently heightened.

SPECIAL EXERCISE FOR PREMATURE EJACULATORS

Only a few years ago, very little could be done to help men who habitually ejaculated within a few moments after entering their wives. This pattern has humiliated men and frustrated women for generations. It is probably the most commonplace sexual problem. Folk remedies such as trying to think of something else (like emptying the garbage, or counting backward from two thousand by sevens) never worked. Wearing a condom or using a desensitizing cream didn't solve the problem either. Today, through the work of J. H. Semans, and of Masters and Johnson, all that is changed. A competent sex therapist can help any couple with this problem in a few weeks. The success rate is about 95 percent.

The technique is not mysterious and if both partners are committed to solving the problem, many couples can achieve good results without professional intervention. Should problems develop in the use of the self-treatment program described below, however, it is good to know that success is still possible through professional assistance.

STAGE 1. *Learning Extravaginal Control.*

This exercise has some things in common with Stage 2 in the previous exercise. Sexual intercourse is forgone for the period of the exercise and the focus is on genital pleasuring. The wife does all the pleasuring in this case, however, and the roles are slightly altered because the goal is a little different.

In this exercise, she stimulates his genitals—without using any lotion or lubricant—until he feels almost ready to ejaculate. Then he has her stop for a while until the feeling passes and the erection subsides a little. Then she begins again. The process is repeated several times per session until, by common consent, she finally does not stop, but lets him come to a climax. The husband's job in these sessions is to concentrate all his attention on the sensations she is producing. He is to become an expert on every shade of feeling in his penis so that he can tell exactly how far he is from an ejaculation. At first, he may misjudge occasionally and have an unscheduled orgasm. When this happens, of course, it ends the session. But gradually he will grow more and more expert at knowing just when to tell his wife to stop stimulating. This technique will make him proficient enough to have complete control when ejaculation occurs. As he becomes more sure of himself, he will also find that he can enjoy a longer and longer period of stimulation before giving the signal to stop.

An alternative developed by Masters and Johnson is the "Squeeze Technique." This involves the wife's not only stopping stimulation at the critical point, but also grasping the penis firmly between her thumb and two fingers, just behind the head, and squeezing hard for about ten seconds. This guarantees that no ejaculation can occur and immediately reduces the erection by about one-third. The penis is tough and cannot easily be damaged by squeezing, so there need be no fear of harm. The advantage of this technique is that it eliminates unintended ejaculations and speeds up the exercise a little. The advantages of the first approach, which just stops stimulation, is that it is less intrusive and, some feel, effects a better transfer from Stage 1 to Stage 2, which involves learning intravaginal control. Both approaches work. Personal preference should dictate which is chosen.

When control has been established under "dry hand" conditions, the wife should begin using a little lotion or soap on her hand. Most men find this more exciting because it is more like the intravaginal experience. Accordingly, they once again find control difficult to begin with. But when it is fully established under these more challenging circumstances (using the same techniques already described) the couple are ready to move on to Stage 2.

STAGE 2. *Learning Intravaginal Control*

At this point the exercise calls for the man to lie on his back and his wife to kneel astride him in a face-to-face position. After she has stimulated him to produce a sufficient erection, she should place the penis in her vagina and let it rest there for a moment. If he finds this too stimulating, she should remove it until the sensations cease (or remove it and use the squeeze technique). She then proceeds gradually once again, increasing the amount of vaginal movement and stopping on cue as necessary. Within a few sessions, it should be possible for him to gain full control in this position—that is, to maintain the erection as long as they wish. As confidence grows, the "rest" periods will become shorter and less frequent.

When control has been achieved in this position, the couple may want to try the side-by-side position described as option C in the previous exercise.

The final and most demanding position of all is the traditional male-on-top position. This should be attempted only after full control has been firmly established in other positions.

With any luck at all, this exercise should bring about a full resolution of the problem in three, or at the most four, weeks. As I previously mentioned, if it does not, you may wish to seek professional help.

Probably the most frequent difficulty in carrying out these exercises is caused by interruptions due to circumstances (illness, business trips, the wife's period). Another common problem is the wife's becoming impatient and resentful at having to perform this service for her husband while getting very little out of it herself. If she is already resentful and sexually frustrated because of his premature ejaculation, she may find it especially hard to make such an additional investment cheerfully. If this is the case, the couple should discuss the matter fully, using the techniques described in earlier chapters. It may help her to remember that at the end of the exercise, her husband will more than likely be able to meet her sexual needs better than ever before, extending the period of intercourse to any length they mutually agree upon.

THE KEGEL EXERCISE FOR IMPROVING VAGINAL TONE

This exercise was named after Dr. Arnold Kegel, a San Francisco physician who worked with women who had difficulty retaining their urine. They complained of leakage from the bladder at inopportune and embarrassing times—when they sneezed or were extremely tired, for example. He reasoned that in such cases, the sphincter muscle that controls the opening from the bladder must be weak, and he gave them the assignment of exercising this muscle, tightening and releasing it thirty to fifty times morning, noon and evening. Initially, he instructed them to perform this exercise while on the toilet, but he and they quickly discovered that it could be done anywhere: standing on the street, sitting at a desk, riding in an automobile or watching television. In four to six weeks, most women reported a major improvement in their condition. A couple of them also revealed that their sex life had improved dramatically.

This unexpected side effect caused Dr. Kegel to reflect that the same muscle which controlled the opening from the bladder also controlled the opening of the anus and the vagina. It is the pubococcygeal muscle, attached to the pubic bone in front and to the coccyx, or tailbone, in back.

Many clinicians have observed (and many women have discovered) that when this muscle is in good tone, it is a much more lively and rewarding partner to the penis and is also able more adequately to play its role in female orgasm (which consists, in large part, of the involuntary spasm of this muscle).

Obviously, the muscle also plays a crucial role in child-birth, since it is the last orifice through which the child must pass on its way to the outside world. All childbirth-preparation classes include exercises for this muscle. Probably every sexually active woman could profit from a six-week program of Kegel exercises to tone up this muscle at the entrance to the vagina.

As with exercises for any other muscle, especially if it is in flabby condition to begin with, one needs to proceed gradually. Each individual will be able to tell whether thirty contractions per session, three times a day, is too much or too little to start with. By the end of four to six weeks most women could comfortably do one hundred per session.

MAKING LOVE VERSUS HAVING SEX

Some readers may complain that this chapter has dealt primarily with what might be called the technical side of sex: erections, orgasms, muscular competence, timing and so forth. They may feel that the emotional aspects have been largely ignored and perhaps go on to note that the trouble with the modern approaches to sex is that they focus on performance, something that can be rated on a scale from 1 to 10. Where, they ask, is the tenderness, the romance, the commitment? Where is the love?

First, it should be acknowledged that the affectional dimension transcends all the rest. It is a profound truth that technical consideration aside, sex is most rewarding when it is part of a caring, enduring relationship. While this point has not been made explicit in the preceding sections, those who try the exercises will discover that they both require and promote a great deal of affection, respect and trust. But beyond that, if successful they may materially undermine some of the chief enemies of love, such as feelings of inadequacy, frustration and resentment. In my experience, any couple who succeed in making bad sex good or good sex better enhance their entire relationship—not only because an important area is improved but because they have accomplished something of value together.

9

FIDELITY OR INFIDELITY?

It is a sign of our times that arguments for fidelity as one of the foundations of a successful marriage are considered passé in many quarters. My convictions in this matter, however, are strengthened by twenty years of experience with couples who have faced the challenge of infidelity. Accordingly, I want first to spell out the case for fidelity as I see it; second, to give some guidelines for preserving fidelity; and finally, to suggest a few strategies for dealing with infidelity when it occurs.

THE CASE FOR SEXUAL FIDELITY

Since there are so many contradictory voices on this matter today, it may be helpful to sort out the key issues and speak to each one separately. For this purpose, I find the research on Levels of Moral Reasoning by Harvard psychologist Lawrence Kohlberg especially helpful.

He has found that children go through a series of developments as they grow toward moral maturity. They begin with self-centered, hedonistic concerns; they progress next to what Kohlberg calls "conventional morality"; and provided they do not stall at one of these earlier levels, they move ultimately to a "morality of internalized values." According to his studies, this sequence is not restricted to our own culture but occurs universally. Moreover, it seems that the same developmental sequence applies to all moral issues—including, presumably, the issue of sexual fidelity.

Kohlberg lists a total of six stages in the development of moral reasoning:

STAGE 1: Moral decisions are based on the avoidance of pain or other unpleasant consequences.
STAGE 2. Moral decisions are based on the achievement of personal advantages, satisfaction or advancement.
STAGE 3: Moral decisions are based on the approval of others and on the achievement and maintenance of popularity, reputation, admiration, etc.
STAGE 4: Moral decisions are based on conformity to the demands of legitimate authorities such as the state or the church.
STAGE 5: Moral decisions are based on individual commitments which are freely entered into with persons or institutions.
STAGE 6: Moral decisions are based on conformity to internalized, integrated principles (such as the Golden Rule).

While neither this nor any other analytic framework can of itself provide answers to moral questions, it can help us consider how the question of infidelity is faced by persons who find themselves at these various levels of moral development.

STAGE 1. The arguments against marital fidelity used by people at this level are that it is dull, boring, stultifying and unnatural to limit one's sexual activity to one partner. There is no question, of course, that there are marriages in which sex has become monotonous and unrewarding. The need for a remedy is often quite clear. What is not clear is why the remedy cannot lie in revitalizing the stagnant marriage rather than in further endangering its life by infidelity.

As a marriage and family counselor, I am impressed with the genuineness of the pain involved in marital boredom. But I am more impressed with the pain, the mistrust, the hurt, the shame, the guilt and the feeling of being torn apart which are nearly always associated with the discovery of infidelity. There is no more distressing and divisive event in the relationship between a man and a woman than the disclosure that one partner has betrayed the trust of the other. In my view, even at this most primitive level of moral decision-making, the weight of reason lands on the side of fidelity.

STAGE 2. Perhaps the foremost arguments against fidelity at this level are the simple hedonistic ones such as "Why should I deny myself pleasurable experiences?" More sophisticated Stage 2 arguments include "Extramarital sexual involvement will add zest and tone to my life and make me a better, happier mate to my spouse."

I do not deny that some people apparently "blossom" under the stimulus of a rewarding extramarital affair. But as long as this "blossoming" takes place under the perpetual risk of painful discovery, it seems to me that it is merely fool's gold.

My major contention about the Stage 2 argument, however, is that the really rewarding, if less highly touted, experiences in life are to be found in trusting and enduring relationships. Security and stability, integrity and inner peace, certainty of another person's commitment—these are the profoundly satisfying things. Nothing in such relationships inhibits personal growth or spiritual openness. Erik Erikson suggested that in a child's development, basic trust is the foundation upon which independence and every other outreaching quality is based. I believe the same is true of marriages.

STAGE 3. At this level, the touchstone of moral decision-making is the approval of others. One's choice of associates, accordingly, becomes a major determinant of behavior. In effect, a Stage 3 person delegates to others the care and keeping of his marital vows. Proponents of extramarital adventurism who operate at this level generally argue in one of two ways. Their first rationale is that everyone else is doing it— everyone, at least, who is knowledgeable, "with it," "up to date" or not "hung up." To remain faithful, therefore, is to risk being subjected to ridicule and, beyond that, to feeling discriminated against and left out of the main action. The second rationale is based on the fear of being rejected or disapproved of by the accomplice in infidelity. Anyone who makes an outside lover the most significant person in his life discovers that saying "no" is not easy.

At this level of moral reasoning there is no counter-argument other than to point out that one's spouse is also a significant person who has some interest in the issue, and whose approval ought to be valued at least as highly as that of others.

STAGE 4. If the arguments at Stage 3 support infidelity because other people are doing it, the arguments at Stage 4 usually proceed in a different direction. The church, the state and other moral authorities have historically supported sexual fidelity in marriage, particularly in Judeo-Christian cultures. In contemporary society, however, these traditional supports have become less firm: witness the states that have removed "victimless" crimes such as adultery from the statutes.

The arguments for infidelity at this level are based on a preference for new moral authorities who challenge the traditional concept of fidelity as the only approved style of marriage. Perhaps the most widely publicized of these attacks have come from the existential wing of the mental-health field, in which the freedom to choose sexual involvements independently of marriage has become a major moral principle. This principle is also espoused by some advocates of the women's movement who feel that societal prohibitions against adultery were rooted in the concept that women were chattels and must therefore be jealously guarded lest they turn into damaged goods. As proof, they cite the fact that men have never been held to the same standards of fidelity as women.

With this last point—that what is good for the gander is good for the goose—I of course agree. However, I feel that both would profit from honoring their commitments to each other.

As for the more general question, I find it difficult to invest these new "authorities" with the same credibility as the laws and codes of the thousands of societies which have condemned infidelity. I believe that traditional moral prohibitions are founded upon certain fundamental truths about human relationships. Among these are the principles that no society can function without the expectation that social contracts will be honored, and that no social contract is of any value unless the fidelity of the partners to the contract is required.

STAGE 5. If one's moral development has advanced to this level—at which commitments freely made are the sole guide to behavior—there can be no argument for infidelity. It has been asserted, however, that if one is free to make a covenant, one should also be free to renegotiate it. Advocates of this position argue that it is unreasonable and unjust to hold mature men and women to a commitment they entered into as callow youths lacking any real sense of what life would be like as the years progressed.

The flaw in this argument is that in the case of infidelity, the covenants are seldom renegotiated; they are unilaterally broken. Even in those marriages in which adultery is practiced by mutual consent, one partner—most often the wife—is initially coerced into the "swapping" in order to provide her husband with a ticket to the "game."

STAGE 6. Governing one's life by the principles of Stage 6—by an integrated, internalized master principle, such as the Golden Rule—would seem to me to preclude any act that is potentially devastating to another person. Although I have seen the devastation that infidelity can bring, I have never come across anyone who has been destroyed by fidelity.

For all these reasons, I judge marital fidelity to be of great value to individuals, to couples, to families and to the entire social fabric. But in particular, I find it to be the cornerstone of successful marriage.

GUIDELINES FOR PRESERVING FIDELITY

This section is adressed to couples who are fully committed to the principle of fidelity and are prepared to consider how best to preserve this important element in their marriage. Over the years, I have listened to the explanations of dozens of individuals who, despite such a commitment, found themselves involved in adulterous relationships. Again and again, their stories revolve around three issues which I have come to think of as the three R's of infidelity: *Resentment, Rationalization* and *Rendezvous*.

Resentment

The resentment that leads an individual into an adulterous relationship can be based on anything. Typically, though, the failure to find adequate means of dealing with marital resentments is the real root of the problem. One or both partners may lack internal permission even to acknowledge bad feelings. Perhaps the most important single preventive of adultery is a developed and well-oiled mechanism for dealing with strain in the marriage. Earlier chapters in this book deal extensively with how such a mechanism can be constructed and what is involved in its maintenance.

As one might expect, sexual conflict is frequently one of the elements in such resentments. Men and women enter marriage with high expectations of what their affectional life together will be. All too often they are disappointed. Instead of the identity-fulfilling, pair-affirming experiences they anticipated, they encounter insensitivity, excessive demands, lack of response, neglect, rejection. And if they experience these feelings over a sufficient period of time, they may well find themselves ripe for a new relationship which promises them the missing reciprocity, tenderness and fulfillment.

The observation that a sexually satisfying marriage is the best defense against extramarital temptation is not a new one. The author of the Book of Proverbs expressed it poetically when he wrote:

My son, attend unto my wisdom,
And bow thine ear to my understanding:
For the lips of a strange woman drop as an honeycomb,
and her mouth is smoother than oil:
But her end is bitter as wormwood,
Sharp as a two-edged sword.

. . .

Drink waters out of thine own cistern,
and running waters out of thine own well

Let thy fountains [not] be dispersed abroad,
and rivers of waters in the streets.
Let them be only thine own,
And not strangers' with thee.
Let thy fountain be blessed:
And rejoice in the wife of thy youth.

. . .

Let her breasts satisfy thee at all times;
And be thou ravished always with her love.

(PROVERBS 5:1, 3-4, 15-19)

Rationalization

For a person who is committed to the concept of fidelity, getting into an adulterous situation almost always involves rationalization. In the simplest case, he may simply refuse to acknowledge that he is setting himself up for something. For example, a wife may flirt and engage in escalating erotic banter with someone she finds attractive, all the while telling herself and others that it means nothing. Or a husband may get himself into a tempting situation, perhaps while using inhibition-reducing drugs such as alcohol or marijuana, and deny that anything could possibly come of it.

But by far the most interesting and seductive form of rationalization is that which is rooted in virtue rather than vice. I am convinced that more people get themselves into the pain of infidelity through empathy, concern and compassion than through any base motive. The world is full of lonely and vulnerable people, hungry for a sympathetic ear and a shoulder to cry on. With a little help from rationalization, the sympathy leads smoothly into tenderness, the tenderness to the need for privacy, the privacy to physical consolation and the consolation straight to bed. And, as I suggested above, the rationalizations come easier to someone who himself is already starved for affection or full of self-pity.

Obviously, the world would be a poorer place if no one

dared extend understanding and sympathy to a suffering fellow human being for fear of slipping into infidelity. To be fair to yourself and to your marriage, however, you should ask yourself some questions:

1. Is my marriage currently in good repair? Are my most important affectional and sexual needs met within it? Do I feel warm, loyal and sexually attracted to my spouse? If there are problems between us, are we working together constructively to solve them, or are we letting resentments accumulate?
2. Do I find this other person attractive? Does he or she make me feel warm and giving? Do I find myself wishing that I could compensate this good person for all the hurt, pain and deprivation suffered at the hands of others? Would I feel the same way about someone who was twenty years older and a hundred pounds heavier and had a spouse who collected guns?
3. Do I feel that in order to be of real help to this person it is important for us to spend long hours together discussing his or her problems? Do I find myself relating my own marital problems in these sessions? Do I look forward to these sessions and think about this person's problems when we are apart? Has he or she begun to assume a predominant place in my emotions? Do I find touching this person an important part of our relationship?
4. Does my spouse know where I am and what I am doing when I am with this person? If so, does that knowledge lead to approval or disapproval? Why are we not helping this person as a couple?

Rationalization is never more powerful than when it is linked with compassion and kindred virtues. But an honest evaluation of the issues raised by these four sets of questions should give anyone advance warning that a particular relationship may be headed in a dangerous direction. Painful experience shows that the longer you postpone looking clearly at these situations and doing something about them, the tougher it is.

Rendezvous

A rendezvous is a meeting or an appointment to meet. Obviously, infidelity depends upon rendezvous, if it is to occur at all. Yet there is a crucial intermediate step between meeting and cheating. Uncomplicated friendships as well as affairs grow because two people find themselves brought together by circumstances. It is the management of such meetings that determines whether friendship or an affair will be the order of their relationship. Experience suggests that the most difficult situations are those which bring together a man and a woman of similar interests for prolonged periods of time. As the relationship develops into an affair, rendezvous may well be planned; but I am impressed by how often, in the early stages, they occur simply because no one plans to avoid them: that is, they just happen.

I am not talking about single, chance encounters. What I have in mind is the kind of systematic association that coworkers or neighbors experience. There is hardly anyone who, if he makes no effort to manage these relationships wisely, cannot find himself at least potentially overinvolved. Half a dozen examples chosen at random from some recent cases will illustrate the point.

CASE 1. Husband and secretary assigned him by company. They often had to work together on projects and reports. They also ate lunch together (dinner too, on late nights) and commuted together.

CASE 2. Wife and next-door neighbor. He worked a night shift and was home while her husband was at work.

They both loved gardening, began their association over the hedge and then continued it over coffee at his place while his wife was away at frequent church meetings.

CASE 3. Husband and wife's closest friend. The wife asked her to stay in the spare bedroom and take care of the family while she was in hospital having her fifth child in eight years.

CASE 4. Wife and fellow student. They met together for long hours of study, debate and shared interests.

CASE 5. Husband and business partner. They worked together every day, had lunch together, traveled on short (not overnight) trips together.

CASE 6. Wife and co-worker in religious-education program. Both were enthusiastic volunteer youth leaders for their church. They spent hours together planning programs and discussing individual young people and their problems.

It is true that in each of these six cases, the marital relationships involved had a background of resentment and rationalization. Yet none of these people went looking for an extramarital involvement, and it is my belief that not one of these infidelities would have occurred if the individuals concerned had managed the situation more responsibly.

Experience has shown that it does not work if one spouse tries to regulate the other in this matter. Invariably, that just leads to resentment and the charge of being mistrusting, uptight, dirty-minded or paranoid. To avoid this, each individual ought to monitor his own relationships. If you find yourself in a situation involving a delicious privacy with an attractive member of the opposite sex, you should begin to look for ways to restructure the situation. No doubt you will think of a dozen reasons why it is unreasonable to go out of your way to avoid perfectly legitimate and innocent companionship; but then, that may simply mean you need to review the three R's of infidelity one more time.

SURVIVING INFIDELITY AND GROWING FROM THE EXPERIENCE

Having said that almost nothing could be more destructive to a relationship than infidelity, I must now admit that even such painful experiences can be turned to profit for the couple. It may be helpful, therefore, to discuss the main issues that make the difference between success and failure in dealing with this challenge.

Confession

It is said that confession unburdens the soul. Doubtless this is true, but it should not be forgotten that while you are unburdening one soul you are also burdening another. Therefore, you ought to choose circumstances of confession that move the relationship forward rather than backward. On the one hand, if there has been a strain in the relationship which has been sorely felt by the "injured" party but not clearly understood, your acknowledgment may make it possible to clear the air and get down to genuinely open communication in the marriage itself. It is reasonable to expect this unwelcome information to produce various degrees of anger and anguish, but often there is an element of relief also. When someone senses a threatening and inexplicable change in the marital relationship but cannot find a reason for it, his confusion becomes a painful burden in its own right. Ending the deception opens channels of communication that may have been closed.

But on the other hand, confession also prompts many hard questions. Some are unanswerable. How could you have done this to me? How can I ever trust you again? What did I ever do to deserve this? Others are answerable, but full of booby traps. Who is this person? Do you love her? When exactly did all of this happen? Where did you go? What did you do together? How much did you enjoy it? Was it better than with me? Did you use our special love words? Did you talk about us? Did you take precautions against pregnancy? V.D.? Who knows about it? What lies have you told me?

Depending on the circumstances, it might be wise to answer some of these; but demands for clinical sexual details should be resolutely resisted. In response to an informed spouse's assertion of the right to know "everything," repentant mates all too often supply details so vivid and concrete that they can scarcely be set aside. Months and years later they flash into memory, triggered by a date, a place, a word, a circumstance—and they lose none of their power to hurt. It is natural, of course, to be morbidly curious about such things, and injured spouses may argue that nothing could be worse than their fantasies. They are mistaken. Fantasies fade; but sharply etched visions of certified reality live on and on.

When infidelity is turned into a profitable experience by a couple it is because a combination of two things occurs: 1) despite marital hurts and resentments, there is a fundamental commitment to the marriage; and 2) through the terrific jolt which the infidelity and the discovery caused, the couple take a new hard look at their relationship and what they can do to revitalize it.

Counseling can be helpful. I would hope, too, that the concepts and exercises in this book would be helpful. But the couple themselves bear the main burden: choosing to grow together rather than apart in response to an unhappy challenge to their marriage.

10

REMARRIAGE

One of the most cheering facts about modern marriage is that despite the rising divorce rate, people do not seem to have lost faith in marriage itself. I mentioned at the outset that about 80 percent of those who divorce remarry within a few years; I should add here that no matter what the reasons for ending first marriages, second marriages have an almost equal chance of success. This suggests that perhaps as many people learn from their mistakes as repeat them.

Another bit of encouraging information comes from a study I made of stepchildren. As a group, they fared as well as children of similar social class, religion and age who came from "unbroken homes." The study compared the two groups on the basis of school performance, school citizenship, self-esteem, number of same-sex friends, number of opposite-sex friends—and found no differences.

All of this is a tribute to the reconstituted families. Many of them overcome their difficulties and foster sound human relationships. There is no point in pretending, however, that remarriages don't have to cope with problems above and beyond those of first marriages. In dealing with these special problems, I find it helpful to categorize them in terms of either Triangles or Ghosts. Some examples from actual interviews conducted by Dr. Lucile Duberman will make clear what I mean.

TRIANGLES

"My little boy is not allowed to come here. I can't have him in the company of my wife or her children. This is at my ex-wife's request. She's a very hard individual. If I tried to compel her to do this, with an attorney or something, she would do everything in her power to alienate my boy. She's capable of anything and I'm not willing to risk it. I'm hoping in time—and I'm sure it will take a great deal of time—she will allow this."

"She is always making it up to her kids because she divorced their father. I think she feels guilt for their sake. Anyway, there's nothing I can do about it. I like them and all, but they aren't my kids. Besides, I think my wife's kids resent me. I don't know why. They're not real fond of their father and I've really tried to take the place of their father. I think none of us really knows where I stand with them."

"Our biggest problem is my children. I think there are times when my wife thinks I devote too much time to them. When you see them once a week, you don't discipline them as if you lived with them; and there's a tendency to try to pack a lot of attention and love into a short time."

"The relationship between her children and my children is bad because the hostility from my children, especially my daughter, comes out in many different ways. She resents the fact that my stepdaughters live with me and that she lives in a smaller house and that her mother is difficult, to say the least."

Triangles, as illustrated in these excerpts, are situations in which a remarried person is caught between two people who have conflicting demands. In the first excerpt, it is a case of a man trying to maintain a positive relationship with his son while dealing with the hostility of his former wife. In the second case, a man and his new wife are having difficulty over his relationship with her children. In the third, he feels torn between his new wife and the children of his former marriage; and in the fourth, he finds himself caught in the crossfire of his own children who don't live with him and his stepchildren who do. Nor is that the end of the list of possible triangulations. It would not be uncommon for a divorced man who married a divorced woman to find himself enmeshed in a network of at least twelve dilemmas. He could be torn between:

1. former wife—current wife.
2. children of his new marriage—children of his former marriage.
3. children of his former marriage—children of current wife's former marriage.
4. children of new marriage—children of current wife's former marriage.
5. former wife—children of his former marriage.
6. former wife—children of new marriage.

7. former wife—children of current wife's former marriage.
8. current wife—children of her former marriage.
9. current wife—children of new marriage.
10. current wife—children of his former marriage.
11. children of his former marriage—former wife's new husband.
12. children of current wife's former marriage—father of those children.

The figure below illustrates the network of demands upon him. A similar chart could be drawn for the divorced, remarried woman. Her problems are at least as great.

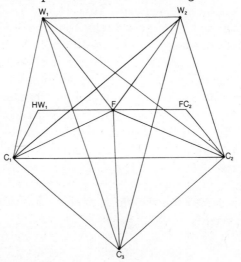

F = Father
W₁ = His former wife
W₂ = His current wife
C₁ = Children of father's former marriage
C₂ = Children of current wife's former marriage
C₃ = Children of father's current marriage
FC₂ = Father of current wife's children
HW₁ = Current husband of former wife

Faced with these difficulties, people can seek three different solutions, depending on their personal styles and their estimate of the situation. I call these the negotiated solution, the imposed solution and the philosophical solution.

The Negotiated Solution

In order to negotiate a solution, it is necessary for each of the three parties involved to rise above petty vindictiveness to a level of enlightened self-interest. It is not necessary to feel warmly affectionate toward every one of the other parties, but it is necessary for each person to trust the others to keep their part of the bargain once it is arrived at. Emotional space is at a premium in these situations, and so must be carefully managed.

Consider the following case. Mary and John had been married sixteen years and had a fifteen-year-old son and a thirteen-year-old daughter. After a number of years, John became involved with Debbie, a divorcee who had three young children. Eventually, he divorced Mary and married Debbie. Mary was given custody of the children and was also awarded the house—which she supported with the salary from her job and John's regular child-support payments. But she felt hurt when John arranged to exercise his alternate-weekend privileges by taking the two children camping with him—something they had done as a family ever since the children were small. He and the children enjoyed it, but she stayed home alone feeling abandoned and miserable. Debbie also became jealous of these trips. Though she had no taste for camping herself, she felt left out of an important and valued part of his life. Even the children and John eventually became less enthusiastic about the trips because of the bad feelings they caused in the two women. Yet no one could think of a better visiting arrangement. The children did not enjoy staying with their stepmother, and no one felt comfortable if John visited his old home for any extended period. Camping was inexpensive fun, and it provided exactly the opportunity for closeness with his children that John wanted.

After considerable discussion with Mary, with Debbie and with the children, John finally proposed the following as a solution:

1. He and his children would continue to go camping, but only once a month instead of every other weekend (for one thing, the weather was getting colder).
2. On the other visiting weekends, they would do something that did not take them away for such an extended period.
3. On the weekends they did go camping, Mary agreed to get out of the house herself (often she visited her parents, a couple of times she went to a health spa to lose weight and once she went to a special art workshop that interested her). For the most part, she found she was able to avoid feeling abandoned or sorry for herself.
4. For Debbie and her own children, John proposed to arrange a monthly special event of some sort that would be a "big deal," thus taking some of the sting out of the "big deal" weekend with the other family. For various reasons, this part of the project was only partly successful, but it reduced Debbie's objections to the camping weekends enough to keep her from spoiling those occasions for John.

The key to making this negotiation work was that John himself undertook actively to solve the problem, rather than just sit back and berate the two women for spoiling his time with his children.

In another case, Lucille, a widow with two boys aged six and four, married Alan, a divorced man with a twelve-year-old girl and a nine-year-old boy. Alan's children lived with their mother for the first year, but her increasingly evident alcoholism led to a general agreement that they should join their father and stepmother. Lucille felt good about the move, and in fact pushed for it. She liked the children and felt they were being neglected at their mother's house. She was sure she could give them the love and guidance they needed.

Things went badly almost from the start. Although they had been reasonably respectful of her and her property when they had visited, when they became permanent members of the family they arrogated to themselves rights and privileges which she resented. They freely raided the refrigerator, which until then had been her exclusive domain. They played their records on her expensive stereo equipment. They watched television at full volume day and night, imposing their undeveloped tastes upon the rest of the family. They fought going to bed. They persisted in taking their snacks into the living room despite her orders to keep all foods in the kitchen. Their table manners and personal hygiene were sorely deficient, and they didn't seem to realize that the younger children were not used to being pummeled or "tickled" punitively (and, from her point of view, brutally). But as upsetting as all of this was, she felt she might have made some progress in dealing with it if Alan hadn't consistently sabotaged her efforts. He refused to enforce her rules when she was gone, and he frequently complained in front of the children that she ought to relax and not get so uptight about everything.

In light of all this, she found herself constantly feeling angry and resentful and, at the same time, guilty at being such a "failure" as a wife and stepmother.

Finally, she got Alan to agree to a conference in order to work things out. They managed to get all four kids to bed early that night, and she presented him with her feelings. She knew it was crucial not to attack him or blame him for everything, because this would have pushed him into a fight-or-run position. Instead, she outlined the situation as a problem they needed to work out together. She asked him if he had any suggestions. He said maybe she was too particular about many things and the kids just couldn't get used to the change from being allowed to do pretty much as they pleased. This was not the kind of suggestion she was hoping for, but she replied that there probably were some areas in which her standards were more rigid than they needed to be. There were, however, other areas in which they both agreed the children needed limits and guidelines. Together, they worked out a set of rules they could agree to. Her original list of twenty-eight was finally boiled down to ten—on the ground, as he put it, that "ten had been enough for God." Each rule had a consequence attached to it. Initially, all the consequences were negative—losses of privilege if the rules were violated; but the final list included a few rewards for conformity and good behavior. As a final step, they agreed to discuss the list with the children rather than simply announce it to them.

The list they presented to the children included the following four items:

1. Refrigerator rules: items that could be freely used as snacks would be marked with a red tag. All other items were off limits without special permission. Violations would lead to loss of all snack privileges for twenty-four hours.
2. All meals and snacks were to be eaten in the kitchen–dining room area. The television set would be moved so that it could be viewed through the kitchen door. Violations would lead to loss of all snack privileges for twenty-four hours.
3. Television watching would be limited to two hours a day on school days and three hours a day on weekends. Violations would lead to a loss of television privileges for the following day (even if it was a weekend).
4. Differences between the younger and older children were to be dealt with without "tickling" or punching on either side. Perfect compliance with this rule for an entire week would result in a parental contribution to their pop-record fund. (This had replaced a punishment for noncompliance.)

The children argued for additional television hours when there was something "special" on. Lucille felt that sixteen hours a week was plenty of watching, but had no objection to their redistributing the hours (borrowing from other days) to accommodate special programs. With only a few other objections, the children accepted the rules. Part of the reason was probably that their father took a firm stand with Lucille on each item. Another important factor was that the rules were presented without accusations or threats.

Each of the individuals involved, given enough emotional space in which to maneuver, rose to the occasion, and the family members became fellow problem-solvers instead of antagonists. This approach worked, of course, because the communication and problem-solving skills discussed in earlier chapters were present to a high degree. Nevertheless, almost any effort of this sort has a better-than-even chance of succeeding. People often respond to a genuinely conciliatory move with more statesmanship than anyone would have imagined.

However, when feelings are so negative that a negotiated solution does not seem possible, the situation is still not desperate. It may simply be time to try:

The Imposed Solution

It is probably inherent in the nature of all imposed solutions that they tend to be self-serving. Sometimes this is true because the imposing party is insensitive to the needs of the other members of the triangle. For example, a father may elect to solve a hassle over child support by moving and leaving no forwarding address. This relieves the pressure on him, but it is definitely irresponsible (not to mention illegal). But even with people of goodwill, human nature is such that each of us views contested issues from a different perspective. If there is no process of negotiation (as in the previous section), it is likely that imposed solutions may not be equally agreeable to all parties. Nevertheless, the problems caused by triangles sometimes have to be handled without such negotiation, and it is my observation that any member of a triangle can make important changes in the pattern simply by changing his own behavior. With forethought, imposed solutions need hurt no one—and may actually benefit all just by reducing the amount of conflict.

For example, Philip always asked his new wife, Nancy, to accompany him when he went to visit his children. It was invariably a miserable experience for her, because of the snide comments—and sometimes direct attacks—that the children made on her. Yet her husband said he was uncomfortable "going back to that house alone." After about three such visits, Nancy simply refused to go. She said, "I realize that it's more comfortable for you when I go, but it's better for you to be uncomfortable than for me to be humiliated. I get so upset that it's a problem between us for days after your visit. I hope you can see my side of it—but in any case, I'm not going." This caused some unpleasantness, but it seemed better to her to try to deal with that than to face the totally disruptive hassle of another visit.

Bernice provides another example. She divorced her husband because of his irresponsibility and drinking. But after the divorce, he still intruded on her life with the same kind of behavior when he visited the children. He would show up without prior announcement, demanding his legal right to see the children. Then, as often as not, he would forget all about them and sit around the house sniping at her or trying to get her to come back to him. Finally, when he did take them out, he sometimes drank too much and got them home late. After trying for months to get him to change his behavior through negotiation, she finally issued the following hard-and-fast rules about visitation:

1. He must call a week in advance so that she could plan the week more reasonably.
2. He could pick up the children in front of the house. He was not invited in.

3. He must agree not to drink alcohol while they were with him.
4. He must get them home by eight o'clock.

Violations of these rules would result in her refusing to let him see them the following month. He grumbled at the rules, but in fact abused them only once during the next year.

Imposed solutions can of course be more complex than this, specifying ways of deciding between conflicting demands under various circumstances. For example, Jackie, Bill's new wife, was worried about his attachment to his children by his former wife. She tended to be oversensitive to any situation in which she felt she had to compete with them. After a long period of trying to handle such situations one at a time, Bill finally imposed the following policy:

1. Ordinarily I will visit them only once a month; but if they should really need me for something I consider legitimate, I will do whatever I feel is called for. I'm still their dad. You will have to trust me not to let that get out of hand.
2. I expect to make child payments each month; but if we should get into a financial bind, you come first. Since my ex-wife has remarried, she doesn't really need the money, and I'll be damned if I'll take the bread out of our mouths to put frosting on her cake. So quit worrying about it.

Rules such as these, even though they are unilaterally imposed and somewhat self-serving, still tend to reduce pressures and confusion. At least they clarify one key person's stand on issues. In the absence of a negotiated settlement, they may be the only available avenue for changing the situation and reducing conflict.

Sometimes, however, it happens that even this solution is not available. The issues may be beyond one's power to influence. It is not uncommon, for example, for one party or the other to feel that visitation rights or other matters have been badly structured by the courts. Or a person may discover that a former spouse is doing everything possible to recruit the children as partisans. In such a case, it may be that literally nothing can be done to change the situation. In these circumstances, all that is left is:

The Philosophical Solution

Although this approach is presented as a last resort, it is actually a powerful and widely applicable tool for dealing with problems that defy interpersonal solutions. It involves learning to avoid what psychologist Albert Ellis has called "horriblizing." People horriblize when they react to upsetting circumstances by saying, out loud or to themselves, "This is horrible, terrible, IMPOSSIBLE! It ought not to be! It is unfair and unjust! No one should have to put up with this! I can't stand it! It's unbearable!"

Recently I was in the departure lounge of an airport on a foggy evening when it was announced that because of poor visibility, the airport had been closed and all flights canceled. I was impressed with the performance of two horriblizers in the group of passengers. One, an older woman, began to weep and wring her hands. She moaned aloud that her children would be frantic with worry about her, that she didn't know what to do, that this was a terrible thing to happen, that she had counted on getting home tonight. Why did everything go wrong for her? What had she ever done to deserve this? How could . . . ? The other, a big, blustering man of about forty, grabbed the passenger agent by the lapels and shook him, demanding to be flown to his destination. He had paid for a ticket. He had a confirmed reservation. He had a very important meeting tomorrow morning which he *had* to attend. He would sue. He demanded to be told exactly how they proposed to get him to his meeting, because if . . .

These sound like extreme examples, but only because the horriblizers voiced their feelings publicly. Similar sentiments are just as commonly felt or expressed privately when life presents people with major frustrations.

The philosophical solution is simply to learn to say different things in your head (or out loud). In the same airport, for example, there were "nonhorriblizers" who were saying to themselves and each other, "This is a nuisance, a real inconvenience, but I guess it's not the end of the world. I'd better find out when they think this will clear up, and book another flight. Then I'd better phone the people who were going to meet me."

It is easy to think of examples of horriblizing that occur in remarriage situations. Visitation rights are sometimes unfairly handled; children are used as pawns by a vindictive former spouse; a current spouse is seduced by his or her "ex" on a visit to see the children. These things hurt; they make you feel angry and perhaps impotent. But horriblizing them only causes ulcers and high blood pressure. You can rehearse a rosary of complaints, indulge in self-pity and cheerlead yourself into a major attack of horribilitis—and still have no good effect on your actual situation. More wisely, though, you can accept the facts, acknowledge the hurt and go on with your life. You do this by monitoring the sentences you say in your head, avoiding the ones that build up the horror and focusing instead on thoughts like "I'd give anything if this were not the case; but it is, and I guess I'll have to live with it. There is no point in getting more and more angry and depressed; I need a clear head to think what's best to do."

Many Eastern and Western philosophies address themselves to such frustrations and teach methods—meditation, prayer, special exercises—for handling them. There are virtues in all of these, but I have found that it is also possible for many people simply to decide to change the sentences in their head and then go ahead and do it. It has been said that politics is "the art of the possible." So is life. Learning to do what is possible and let the rest go is learning to live. While it may be "natural" to thrash around in a frenzy of moral indignation, accusation and anxiety, it seems to accomplish little that is good and much that is harmful. It reduces the emotional space of everyone involved, and it clouds the mind at a time when clarity is badly needed. The simple recognition that this is true is often enough to move many to change. But for added help, there is an exercise at the end of this chapter for those who have trouble letting go of their inalienable but unhappy right to horriblize.

GHOSTS

Nothing is more annoying to a remarried person than to be compared with a former spouse. Even favorable comparisons can grate. As one woman said, "When he tells me I'm better to make love to than her, it's like three in a bed: him and me and his memories of her."

And when the comparison is unfavorable, the effect is even worse: "Well, I'll admit Harry wasn't much of a husband, but at least he wasn't tight." Or "Mary had her faults, but in all the years we were married never once did she insult me in front of guests." These comparisons muddy what might well be a valid point in each case: "I feel strongly that we need to increase the household budget"; or "I really felt bad to think that you would say that in front of friends. It's important to me to keep that sort of thing between ourselves."

Often, remarried people worry about how they stack up against former spouses; but even if there is pressure for comparisons, it is wisest to stick to the position that past is past and what matters is us, here and now.

Invoking the ghosts of earlier marriages almost invariably reduces emotional space. No one can compete with a memory, and trying to do so attacks one's space in three ways: expectations are multiplied more by comparison than by almost any other technique; yet the criterion for adequate performance is elusive and nonconcrete; and almost by definition, a put-down is built into every comparison.

With such obvious and persuasive reasons for avoiding comparisons, it is perhaps surprising that comparing is so common. But even if you set aside those cases in which a ghost is trotted out precisely in order to hurt or to retaliate for some wrong received, there are still many instances to account for. People often seem hardly aware that they are doing it. I was seeing a remarried couple with sexual problems recently and the husband, in trying to find an explanation for his lack of sexual response, kept referring to the fact that he had never had any trouble in his two earlier marriages; he just couldn't understand why it was a problem with his wife. She looked pained every time he made these comments, but she said nothing. Finally, I remarked that his references to previous partners sounded to me like a put-down of his present wife. He looked surprised. "I didn't mean anything by it," he said. "It's just that we both want to get to the bottom of this, and the simple truth is that I never had any problems sexually in my former marriages. My first wife was—" I had to interrupt and ask him to spare us the clinical details of how easily he had turned on in his other relationships. No doubt one of his reasons for retailing such information was to establish himself as sexually competent; I believe that, as he claimed, he was not purposely trying to hurt his wife in the process. Yet he placed her in a position in which the only response she could think of was that they were both not as young as they used to be. She did, however, toss in the tidbit that if push came to shove, she had it on good authority that she was not altogether sexually unattractive to men. It was all I could do to get them to call off an incipient wrestling match between ghost and counterghost.

If my experience as a counselor is any guide, there is virtually never a case in which this kind of comparing is either necessary or helpful. Ghosts are lonely, forlorn creatures, and they make miserable company. Don't even whistle when you pass them. Just let them rest.

EXERCISES

My observations show that love can indeed be wonderful the second time around. The following exercises are designed to help remarried couples manage the triangles and the ghosts so that they don't get in the way of that wonder.

1. NEGOTIATING SOLUTIONS TO TRIANGULAR PROBLEMS
   A. Draw a picture of all the triangles you are involved in, similar to the figure on p. 172.
   B. Pick out either the triangle that is causing the most trouble or the one you think would be easiest to work on.
   C. Arrange a meeting with one or both of the other parties to the triangle.
   D. Outline the problem as you see it—clearly, briefly and without blaming anyone. (That is the hard part.)
   E. Proceed on the assumption that none of the parties is happy with the present situation and that all would like to improve it if they could find a solution that would not be against their several interests. (This assumption of goodwill is crucial.)
   F. Invite suggestions from the others and offer some yourself. Use the technique of putting yourself in the other people's places and trying to understand what is most important to them. Check out your understanding of their feelings. Be an active listener and a nonattacking communicator.
   G. If absolutely conflicting interests emerge, suggest compromises on all sides. (But watch your style messages.)

If this program is pursued in a noncompetitive way, you have every reason to expect success. You may even be ready to go on to other, more problematic triangles.

Should this approach fail, though, you may wish to consider the following exercise.

2. IMPOSING SOLUTIONS TO TRIANGULAR PROBLEMS

If the others involved refuse to join with you in finding a solution, it is often possible to approach the problem single-handedly.

A. On a piece of paper, state the problem as clearly as possible.

B. List all your own contributions to the problem. If you cannot think of any, you are probably suffering from a blind spot and may wish to ask a neutral friend for ideas. If you still can't come up with any, go on to Exercise No. 3.

C. For each of your own contributions to the problem, list at least one and preferably two or three alternative ways of acting that might improve matters.

D. Opposite each alternative, write out the changes in the behavior of the other members of the triangle you think it would elicit.

E. Evaluate the cost or benefit to you of these changes (yours and theirs). This is called cost/benefit analysis and is an important element in all effective planning.

To give you an idea of how this might be done, consider a couple of examples:

CASE 1

Matt, a thirty-nine-year-old draftsman, lost his wife of eighteen years in an automobile accident. After a year, he married Liz, a dynamic and beautiful twenty-six-year-old woman he knew from work. His two younger children (ages ten and nine) got along well with her, but his sixteen-year-old, Karen, was locked in mortal combat with her from the moment they met. He thought things would improve, but they only became worse. At first Liz tried to make a go of it despite Karen's rudeness and open defiance, but recently she had decided she was through. Matt found himself in the middle. His paper up to this point looked like this:

Problem: I love Karen and Liz, but they hate each other. Karen shows no respect for Liz, and Liz has become nasty toward Karen. I hate the atmosphere in our home.

What I Do to Contribute to the Problem:

1. Possibly Liz and I are too affectionate in front of the children. Especially lately, I think Liz does this partly because she knows Karen hates it. I have gone along, even though I am feeling more and more uncomfortable with it.

2. I never take sides in their quarrels; I have felt they could work it out best between themselves—but Liz feels I ought to back her up more.

3. I don't spend time alone with Karen anymore. This probably makes her more jealous.

4. Although I have let both of them know how much I hate their quarreling, I have not set down any rules or guidelines about what is tolerable and what is absolutely intolerable. *Alternatives:*

1. We could save the affection for private and see if it would cut down on the problem.

Costs: Liz will say Karen is coming between us and dictating how we do and don't express our feelings to each other.
Benefits: Karen will have fewer bad feelings to deal with.
Balance: Worth a try.

2. Liz and I should get our act together in terms of Karen's rights and responsibilities, and then I should back her up 100 percent.

Costs: Karen will feel I am taking sides against her. I'm afraid she may even do something dumb like run away.

Benefits: Karen is really out of line and needs some guidance. Possibly this would work. Certainly Liz would be pleased.

Balance: Probably should have done it from the beginning. May be tough to start now, but I will try it and see what happens.

3. I could set aside some time to teach Karen to drive. This is something she wants, and it would give us a chance to talk more.

Costs: Liz says Karen is too irresponsible to drive and that she ought to have to earn the privilege. Liz will fight this one.

Benefits: Good chance to talk to Karen alone. Eventually she can run errands and cut Liz's chauffeuring time.

Balance: Liz won't like it, but I'll do it. Perhaps I can use it to teach Karen some responsibility.

CASE 2

Barbara finds that her husband, Harold's, former wife, Susan, is always on the phone asking him to come over and fix things or bail her out of messes she's gotten herself into. She even uses the children as bait. Harold doesn't see through it at all and goes trotting off any time of the day or night on five minutes' notice. Here is Barbara's sheet:

Problem: How to keep Harold home more.

WHAT DO I DO TO CONTRIBUTE TO THE PROBLEM?

1. I let him go. I complain, but I haven't really laid it on the line.

2. I give him her messages.

Alternatives:

1. A. I could tell him that anything over once a week is out! And no calls after 9 P.M.
   B. I could try to get him to move away from here.
   C. I could get a private number.
   D. I could go with him every time and make myself a nuisance (to her, not to him).
2. I could refuse to give him her messages.

Evaluation:

1. B and C are impractical; she'd get our private number from him anyhow. A might work. D might work if A doesn't.
2. Wouldn't work. It would make him too mad.

Having gotten this far in the exercise, you must now move on from analysis and try to translate into action the things you feel have some chance of success. After a suitable period, evaluate your program's effectiveness. Are you getting the results you want? On the basis of that evaluation, consider continuing or reshaping your approach. Such programs may not always be directly successful, but they often stir things up enough to motivate others in the triangle to enter into joint negotiations after all. If nothing else works, consider Exercise 3 below.

3. ACHIEVING THE PHILOSOPHICAL SOLUTION
   A. Write out the problem in brief form.
   B. Write out all the thoughts that go through your head when you think about this problem.
   C. Look over these thoughts, keeping a sharp eye out for horriblizing. Check for oughts and oughtn'ts, shoulds and shouldn'ts, appeals to right and wrong, protestations of injustice or unfairness. Check for statements about how hard it all is to bear, and for overt or covert threats to self and others.
   D. Consciously replace these sentences with less fre-

netic ones—and with more sober analyses of what needs to be done. Do *not* try to lie to yourself with phrases like "I don't really mind; it doesn't really hurt; it will all turn out okay in the end." Instead, take a philosophical stance: "I'll survive; life must go on; I suppose they just don't know any better; it must look different from their perspective; it is regrettable, unfortunate and hurtful, but it is not the end of the world; I don't like it, but I can live with it if I have to."

ON PROFITING FROM EXPERIENCE

Beyond the specific skills I hope to teach in these exercises there is another capacity that in my experience makes all the difference in second marriages (and in life). It is the ability to grow from painful experience instead of being stunted by it. If there is one thing that an unsuccessful first marriage provides freely, it is pain. What a waste if it embitters and hardens and perpetuates itself instead of fostering increased compassion and understanding. What a loss if the unwelcome opportunities to face unpleasant truths about oneself lead only to better defenses and not to more insight and honesty. How doubly sad if failure fails to teach how to distinguish between issues which should be let go without contest because they don't really matter and those which should be seen through to the end at whatever hazard because they matter above everything else. When love is wonderful the second time around, it is because the experience of the first time around was not wasted.

11

INTERNAL TENSION, EXTERNAL CRISES

SCENE 1

(*Ted and Ann's bedroom twenty-five minutes after they've returned home from the movies. Ted is already in bed, apparently asleep. Ann enters.*)

ANN (*playfully*) You can't fool me, Ted Andrews. You're just pretending to be asleep so you can lure me into your bed all unsuspecting and naive, and then pounce upon me and rob me of my virtue.

TED (*muttering*) Ann, I'm kinda sleepy for that at this point.

ANN Can this be the Theodore Andrews I have known and loved? What's the matter, Ted? You're usually not this hard to seduce.

TED Maybe I expected you twenty minutes ago.

ANN   Well, I'm sorry. Danny woke up when he heard us come in and I had to get him settled.

TED   I just hate always being last in line behind the kids. There is absolutely no reason for Danny to get up this time of night and no reason for you to spend twenty minutes settling him. I got the impression in the car that we were going right to bed when we got home.

ANN   That's not fair. Do you think I planned on Danny waking up? Ted, he's just a baby. He doesn't understand about these things. (*attempting to lighten things up with humor*) I'll tell you what I'll do. Tomorrow I'll have a little talk with him. "Danny," I'll say, "Now that you're three, there are a few things you need to know about what mommies and daddies have in mind after the movies."

TED   I'm sorry—this may be funny to you, but it isn't to me. And it's not just tonight. It's all the time. They always come first.

SCENE 2

(*Patty is in front of the mirror, putting the last touches of makeup on her face. She views the result critically as the telephone rings.*)

DENNIS   Hi, honey. Uh, listen: these negotiations are dragging on, and it looks like I'm not going to make it home till late. The other side wants to get it finished up so they don't have to stay over an extra day. I'm afraid this kind of spoils our date.

PATTY   Dennis! This is not just a date; this is our anniversary. I have the reservations, the tickets. I was expecting you any minute.

DENNIS   Look, I'm sorry. This is not the way I want to spend the evening, believe me. But I don't think you could expect me to tell these guys they'll just have to stay an extra day because I had a date with my wife. Maybe I can get away for a late supper if things go well.

PATTY   I'll bet you didn't say a word when they suggested it. Good old Dennis just smiled and said, "Fine, fine; I wasn't doing anything this evening anyway."

DENNIS   C'mon, honey. These men are anxious to get away tonight if we can wrap it up. What am I supposed to say?

PATTY   I suppose it all depends on who is more important to you. Well, you just take your time. As far as I'm concerned, you can stay all night! (*Slams down phone.*)

SCENE 3

(*Bill is working in the garage on the carburetor of his 1962 Mustang. Sandy enters.*)

SANDY   I just finished talking to Mother. Bill, she's very upset over what you said to her last night.

BILL   (*concentrating on his work*) Uh-huh.

SANDY   You know how she feels about our never going to church, and you shouldn't make fun of her when she tries to talk to us about it. Even if we don't look at it the same way she does, that's no reason to make her feel bad about it.

BILL   Uh-huh.

SANDY   Bill! Will you please do me the courtesy of looking at me when I talk to you?

BILL   In a minute. This is kind of tricky.

SANDY   Sometimes I wish you would just get rid of that old car. It gets more attention than your family does.

BILL   (*without looking up*) Sometimes I feel that way about your mother. Sorry—sorry! Just a little humor there.

One of the universal and never fully resolved tensions of married life is wrapped up in the question "Who comes first, me or them?" On the one hand, all of us expect our spouses to be understanding when they have to take a back seat to other pressing problems or commitments. On the other hand, each of us feels that in any real crunch he ought to come first. It is never clear which of the two conflicting rules should apply in a given situation. Very often each partner chooses the rule that justifies his or her own behavior. One pleads the legitimacy of the investment in the children, the job, the relative, the hobby. The other pleads for the top billing he thought he was guaranteed by the marriage contract.

There is no set of rules or guidelines for determining who is right in these cases. For example, if a couple were to go over the scenes at the beginning of the chapter, there is an even chance that they would disagree about who was right in at least one of them. It is clear that the marriage can't always come first in every case. Life is demanding; there are some sacrifices one must make in order to survive and to honor one's obligations to others. Those who feel threatened by every outside claim on their spouse's time or loyalty are simply being unrealistic. But it is also true that if the marriage comes in last in every competition, it will wither from lack of nourishment.

Finding the balance point that satisfies both partners is often hard. Yet failing to do so leaves at least one of them feeling sulky and undervalued. In fact, it is not at all uncommon for each partner to feel that the other expects an awful lot and yet doesn't return much on the investment.

Perhaps the following checklist will be useful in evaluating the situation in your own marriage. It is best if both partners participate in this exercise, but even one can gain perspective by considering these issues.

1. Make a thoughtful list of those areas of your life in which you feel in direct competition with other important obligations or enthusiasms of your spouse. Specify the situations in which you feel it is all right for him or her to assign number one priority to these other demands. Then list the situations in which coming first really matters to you—situations in which if you are put on the back burner, you feel abandoned and betrayed instead of supported and loved.

Be sure to pay attention to whether your partner is in a "no win" situation. That is, ask yourself if you are testing your spouse's loyalty in areas in which you would be better advised to support his or her fulfillment of legitimate obligations. Try to look at them from your spouse's viewpoint. After chipping away at the list as far as seems reasonable, let your partner know which are the crucial areas of competition for you. If you can't win 'em all, concentrate on winning the ones that really matter. Don't waste energy or morale on secondary issues.

2. Make an equally thoughtful list of those areas of your marital life in which your spouse feels threatened by competing loyalties, obligations and enthusiasms of your own. (If your spouse is willing to cooperate, check your list against his or hers; you may be surprised at some sore points you overlooked.) Specify those situations in which you think the competing demands are legitimate, as well as those in which you feel you could not abandon your commitments honorably or sensibly. These last are where you feel that your spouse should recognize the reality of the circumstance you are in and forgo making a contest. Then specify those situations in which a small investment of sensitivity on your part could reassure your mate of primacy in your life without seriously compromising other important commitments. Often a telephone call, a note or a touch is enough to give the reassurance that your spouse is not being forgotten even though some other demand is occupying the center of your attention.

Be sure to note whether you yourself are taking responsibility for reassuring your mate of his or her importance, and not just acting as if it were something that should be self-evident. Consider also whether you are investing your time and energy equitably in the various sectors of your life that are important to you. In particular, be honest about just how often your marriage comes in second (or last).

3. If your mate is willing to cooperate, share your lists and discuss how you both feel on each issue—without, of course, getting into a lather about it. Use the communication skills taught in earlier chapters. With goodwill, it often takes very little effort to achieve big increases in each partner's feelings of security and importance. Should the discussion deteriorate into a standard quarrel, reread the first few chapters to see if a better mode of discussion cannot be achieved.

A little reflection on the three scenes at the beginning of this chapter will provide insight into how couples can deal with issues of this sort. In Scene 1, for example, the wife might have settled her son Danny with more dispatch, or better still, asked her husband to settle him while she got herself ready for bed.

In the second case, it would probably have been best if the husband had acted more assertively to protect the anniversary celebration. Few events are more heavily loaded with symbolic value. A man (or woman) fouls up on an anniversary only at grave risk to his spouse's morale. In my experience, others will often accept your own definition of a situation provided it is simply stated as a fact and not argued for or self-servingly explained. For example, this husband might have told his out-of-town colleagues early on: "Listen, you fellows should know that if we don't finish by five, we'll have to go over till tomorrow. Tonight's my anniversary, and as you married men know, that is *not* a negotiable clause in the contract." I would bet that in ninety-nine cases out of a hundred they would have accepted his stipulations (with no more mumbling or complaining than they would give to bad weather or a head cold).

In the extraordinary case, in which matters of great moment hang on completing the contract by midnight (averting a strike, missing a deadline for a bid, saving a company from an imminent takeover), the wife should have been warned as early as possible that this might happen, and alternative plans arranged.

In the third case, there was an opportunity for each to make things easier. She could have come in and waited for him to finish the immediate project. He could have told her that he would like to talk to her about it if she could just wait a minute. The issue of the mother-in-law could have been handled better on both sides. On the one hand, the wife found herself rushing in from the telephone call to belabor her husband on her mother's behalf. It seems likely that she might have found her husband more receptive at another time. On the other hand, it is apparent that the husband habitually deals with many issues by joking (making fun of his mother-in-law's ideas about religion, the crack about wishing he could get rid of her instead of his car). Probably a less flip approach to their problems would have been more effective.

COMPETING WITH CRISIS

Part of the traditional wedding ceremony requires that the couple pledge to take each other as husband and wife "for better, for worse; for richer, for poorer; in sickness and in health." The authors of that phrase apparently recognized that one of the chief threats to marital happiness is external misfortune. As one woman put it:

"I think we could handle our marital problems if life would give us half a chance. In the last eighteen months everything has happened to us. The government canceled the project Lew was working on and he was laid off. Then we lost Jody in the car accident. Then I was laid up with the operation on my back. I don't know—it just seems that all the laughing and all the loving has been squeezed right out of us."

In a book like this, it is a temptation to treat all problems as if they were of the couple's own making. Admittedly, such an approach makes it easier for them to see that solutions too are within their joint reach. But it also tends to leave them at sea in that great body of marital troubles caused by "the slings and arrows of outrageous fortune." For one thing, the fates can attack from so many unexpected directions that it seems futile to attempt to defend against every possibility. For another, it seems to be perversely true that, as in the example above, troubles rarely come one at a time. Instead they seem to gang up on a family without giving them a chance to regroup.

Still, the subject cannot be ignored. Whether a couple grow together or apart over the years may well be determined by how they handle the unforeseen crises that inevitably arise. Some seem to weather these things better than others. So far as I can tell, those who succeed do so largely because of two factors: the emotional and material resources they can marshal, and the definition they are able to make of the situation in their own minds.

Resources

This is not a book that addresses itself to issues such as savings and investments and capital and credit. These material resources are of tremendous importance; but the kind of capital I feel qualified to talk about is emotional capital. To some extent this can be stored in the relationship itself; to some extent it can be stored in a network of relatives or close friends. Both resources are invaluable.

When hard times come and there is a loss of health, of income or of a member, or an increase of obligations and demands, some couples are able to draw upon a history of mutual support. Others, however, find themselves forced to deal with the problem from a storehouse of morale already depleted by power struggles, emotional crowding and resentment hoarding. But in addition to the obvious benefits of a good track record, there is one additional quality that really makes a difference: it is flexibility.

The story is told of a young man who was taking a test in college physics. The final question, for 5 points, was "If a man had only a barometer to assist him, how could he use it to estimate the height of a tall building?" What was wanted, of course, was an answer based on the fact that a barometer, because it shows a lower air pressure reading at the top of the building than at the bottom, can be used as a rough kind of altimeter. For his answer, though, the young man wrote, "Actually I can think of two methods. First he could measure the length of the barometer and then, as he walked up the stairs to the top he could measure the height of the building by placing the barometer against the wall and measuring the number of barometer lengths it took to get to the top. Or, more efficiently, he could take the elevator to the top of the building, lower the barometer over the edge on a string until it reached the ground and then measure the string."

When his paper was returned, he got no credit for his answer and thereby missed an "A." He took the paper to the professor and complained that he had actually given two correct answers, not one, and could not understand on what basis the points were withheld. The professor told him that he knew very well that this question was asked on a test in a physics course and that while the height of the building might be estimated in these ways, the student's knowledge of physics could not be. However, he continued, he was a fair-minded man and would be willing to give him the points if he could sit down and write out an answer that showed his mastery of the subject matter covered in the course.

The young man sat down to the task and in a few minutes turned in the following answer:

"I can think of at least three ways the man could estimate the height of the building using the principles we have studied in this course. The simplest would be to use the principle that light travels in a straight line. He could measure the length of the barometer (L) and compare it with the length of its shadow (S) at a given moment in the day. Then he could measure the length of the building's shadow (B) and estimate the height of the building (H) using the formula $H = \dfrac{BL}{S}$

"If the building were very tall, a somewhat more complicated approach would be to suspend the barometer on a string from a tripod and measure very precisely the time it takes to complete one arc on a pendulum. Then repeat the experiment at the top of the building. If the measurements were precise, the difference in time due to the difference in distance from the center of the earth should give an estimate of the height of the building.

"Probably the best way, however would be to drop the barometer over the edge of the building and time its fall. Allowing for the median speed of sound over that altitude range and using the formula for the acceleration of a falling object, this should produce a fairly accurate estimate of the height of the building."

The professor was enraged. "Why," he demanded, "why do you refuse to give me the most obvious answer? I am going to give you one more chance. I want you to tell me once and for all if you had a barometer how you would in fact—actually, sensibly and in real life—use it to discover the height of a tall building. Please spare me your cleverness and give me a straight answer."

"Well," said the student with a sigh, "You are right, of course. In actuality I would not do any of these things. In all honesty I would take the barometer and check it to see that it was registering air pressure properly. Then I would take it to the office of the building superintendent and say,

'If you will tell me the height of this building I will give you this first-class barometer.' "

He did not get the points, but he did demonstrate a flexibility that made the professor look as if he were chiseled out of chalk. Many marriages are more like the professor than the young man. People insist on one and only one correct answer, when in fact there are as many answers as they have ingenuity to imagine. Their narrow insistence is no problem as long as the one rigid answer is effective; but let a crisis arise which nullifies its effectiveness and the rigid family is left crippled, unable to respond in any constructive way. In that circumstance, the members find themselves out of emotional space and either run away or turn on each other.

The more flexible couple, by contrast, will keep reassessing the problem till they come up with a new way of proceeding that works as well or nearly as well as the old way. They may reverse roles—for example, with her going to work and him doing the housework. Or, like one couple I know, they may shift to an entirely different occupation. Glenn and Wilma were jolted out of their comfortable life by a change in his company's management and were left with a mass of payments on their oceanfront property and cabin cruiser. The job market in his field was flooded with applicants. He couldn't even get a nibble in response to his dozens of résumés. But when they ran out of money, did they sell the house and boat and peddle encyclopedias door to door? They did not. They started renting out their boat to sport fishermen, with themselves as crew. Gradually they expanded the business to include two other boats and a marine-accessories shop. At this writing, they are doing well and they have maintained the life-style they love.

A young woman of my acquaintance broke her back in a skiing accident. She became a paraplegic. Her fiancé broke off the relationship and disappeared over the horizon. Many people would have given up on life. Two years later, however, this young woman is mobile again through the use of a motorized wheelchair and special van. She is engaged to another paraplegic she met at the Veterans Hospital while both were being trained to operate a specially designed motor vehicle. They are developing a talking-book business so that handicapped persons who cannot easily handle or read a book can enjoy current best sellers in condensed audiotaped versions. With the help of nonhandicapped friends, they have dinner parties and entertain. I would venture to say that she is as socially active today as she was before the accident. Courage is part of the secret of her success; but of equal importance are ingenuity and mental flexibility. She starts with the premise that there has to be a way to do what she wants to do, and she doesn't give up until she has found it. The approach works just as well for people who have the use of all their limbs.

Besides maintaining flexibility (and courage), a couple can prepare for adversity by keeping a reliable network of relatives and friends within helping distance. Such networks are handy in at least three ways. First, they are there for direct emotional support. They can offer a sympathetic ear, wise counsel and the affirmation of concern. Professionals such as counselors, doctors, lawyers and clergy do a very small part of all counseling. Most of it is done, as it has always been, in the informal network.

Second, they can help directly by fixing meals; baby-sitting; doing housework; providing transportation; lending money, tools, clothes, furniture or whatever is needed. Finally, they can serve as bridges to the resources of the larger community. They provide access to doctors, funeral directors, counselors or housekeepers. They may ferret out a lead to a job or a loan, or to somebody in local government who can intervene on the family's behalf.

It may seem that investing in friends and relatives might be as likely to compete with the marriage as to help it. In the short run, that is sometimes the way it works out. But the evidence is compelling that in the long run the marriage is far more likely to be strengthened than weakened by this network of concern. Couples who live isolated from such ties have the highest divorce rates, the highest incidence of mental illness and suicide, and the most frequent problems with interpersonal violence and child abuse. The network appears then to sustain the family not only in times of external crisis but also when internal strife might otherwise tear it apart.

Defining the Situation

Many things affect the way a couple define a crisis, and most of them are not susceptible to control. One element, however, over which there is some control is the degree of their preparation for disaster. Sometimes life itself prepares a couple: they have been through illness before, so they know what to do when it occurs again. In other cases, the pair can actually anticipate the problem and to a large degree pre-solve some of its most perplexing aspects. One of the most cherished experiences of my childhood was being in charge of fire drills for one semester in junior high school. Once a month I got to call an unannounced fire drill and clock how long it took everyone to get out of the building. When I had checked to see that everyone was out, I then rang the all-clear bell and they could come back. (I never expect to know such a feeling of power again.) We never had a real fire at our school, but if we had, I am confident that we could have emptied the building in under two minutes because we practiced doing it so often.

Some families, wisely enough, have literal fire drills. Depending on the part of the country, others have earthquake drills, flood drills, tornado drills and hurricane drills. Fewer families practice what they would do if Daddy died or if Mother went to the hospital for an extended period. Yet these are at least as likely to occur as any of the natural disasters. Without being morbid about it, I have talked to my family about what it would be like if I died. We have talked about wills, insurance and Social Security, vested retirement funds, savings, college costs and how much money Mother could make per month. We talked about whether they would be able to keep the house or would have to move. We worked through their resistance to their mother's remarrying. We considered what each one would have to do to help the others and to keep the old ship afloat. At the end, I was gratified to hear our teen-ager say, "You know, I didn't think we could make it—financially, I mean—but I added it all up and I think we could." So far, I am pleased to say that I am in good health and intend to raise my family without taking advantage of our advance planning. But if I should die, I am persuaded that my family are better prepared than most to define the situation as survivable. That seems as important to me as a will or an extra insurance policy.

One troublesome element in defining the problem is the tendency some couples have to horriblize and personalize. We discussed this in detail in the chapter on the special problems of remarriage, but it applies equally to any crisis. The same event can be viewed as terrible, horrible and beyond endurance; or, alternatively, it can hopefully be accepted as an unhappy and regrettable misfortune which must be worked through to the best conclusion possible. A death, an illness or a financial reverse can be viewed as a personal affront, or it can be viewed as just one of those things that happen and must be dealt with. The exercise called "The Philosophical Solution" (page 188) is worth reviewing in this context.

Finally, one of the most pernicious tendencies in time of crisis is to try to fix the blame for the whole thing on one's partner. In some cases, one or the other may indeed have been the major contributor to the problem through negligence or bad judgment. If the crisis is not to destroy the marriage, however, it must be defined as a joint problem which both are committed to attack as a team. Perhaps nothing I have written in this chapter makes more difference than this in determining whether the marital commitment itself survives and grows in the face of adversity.

Like most marriages, mine has been through births and deaths, through illness and financial crisis, through the pains of overwhelming commitment and unwelcome moves. And yet we have bobbed up again like a cork in choppy waters. The trick is to avoid turning any of these into a deadlier crisis, a crisis of trust between us. When couples have to grapple with unkept promises, with lying and infidelity, with attack and feelings of betrayal, that is when the ship of matrimony begins to take on water. In every other kind of crisis you can draw upon each other's strength, but in crises of trust one has only one's own depleted inner resources and the sad strength of anger to fall back on.

12

PERSONAL VIEWS ON...

I hope it has been evident throughout this book that I am generally reluctant to provide couples with advice based on my own notions. I prefer to help them develop new skills of their own and master for themselves those basic principles which can resolve their problems. In this chapter, however, I have been prodded to discuss (in a question-and-answer format) my own views on a number of contemporary issues.

QUESTION So far in this book you have largely ducked the issue of divorce. It's clear that you are pro-marriage; but what if the marriage doesn't work out?

C.B I am grateful for divorce, even though many divorces are simply mistakes. People exchange one spouse for another without improving their condition or learning anything in the process. But sometimes a second chance makes all the difference. In my own case, I married well in the first place and expect things to continue to improve as they have been doing for the past twenty-five years. But my mother and my aunt both finally found happiness in their third marriages. I would not wish to live in a time or place where that was not possible.

QUESTION   What about open marriage? Many people believe that traditional, possessive unions are too confining for modern men and women.

C.B.   I am asked that all the time. Over the years I have watched couples try a wide variety of "open" approaches to their marriages. I guess I have finally concluded that open marriage is like a highly advertised fad diet. It promises renewed vitality and boundless energy by providing several times the minimum daily requirements of freedom, variety and growth. As with all such promotions, books are written, testimonials collected, movements launched, regular meetings of the true believers set up. Bedazzled customers are assured that if they still feel empty after using the prescribed diet, it is their own fault. They have not followed the instructions, their attitude has been wrong, their own metabolism is deficient. But as pain multiplies and resentment fails to yield to rhetoric, it finally becomes apparent that the much-advertised supernutriment is lacking in essential vitamins. It seems clear to me that while freedom, variety and growth are essential ingredients in the human diet, so also are safety, trust and stability. People have known this for generations, but sometimes they get excited about the new product and forget.

QUESTION   Along the same line, many couples today are deciding not to have any children. They feel that life holds many rewarding experiences for couples who are not tied down. I know that you and Kathleen have a large family. I'm sure you love your children; but frankly, over the years haven't you ever wished the two of you were free of your obligation to them?

C.B. There are, of course, times when responsibilities toward children cramp a couple's style. But every choice inevitably has implications for other choices. Anyone mature enough to make such a choice should, presumably, be mature enough to accept the costs as well as the benefits of such a choice.

Children have been getting a bad press lately. It's claimed that having a baby puts the marital relationship under strain. NON (the organization for nonparenthood) and some elements of the women's movement have argued that bearing children is the great unequalizer. They hold that if women are to compete with men successfully, they must give it up. Finally, we have all been warned again and again that the world has too many babies as it is. I suppose it is no wonder that young people think twice about becoming parents.

Personally, though, I'm glad to see that the trend toward voluntary childlessness seems to be turning around since its peak in about 1975. In my view, children are the most powerful motivators a couple have to grow up themselves. Having a family forces us to sacrifice, to learn to put another person's needs above our own, to expand our investment in life and in the future. I would not trade my experience as a father for any of my degrees or professional achievements.

QUESTION But some people don't seem to be able to handle the responsibility of children. The incidence of child abuse (not to mention spousal abuse) seems to be growing at a frightening rate. At least, we hear more about it. Don't you think some couples shouldn't have children?

C.B. Possibly. But those are not the ones who are deciding not to. It takes a fair degree of decision-making ability and commitment to avoid becoming parents. The people who abuse children, however, are precisely the ones who are lacking in impulse control. I shall never lose my sense of moral indignation that children are starved and neglected and beaten and sexually abused. Moreover, when they try to get help from other adults they are often not believed or refused help. One young woman told me that when she was about thirteen her father began to force his sexual attentions on her. One day in Sunday school the lesson was on honoring your father and your mother. She took her courage in her hands and asked, "But what if they want you to do something bad?" Her teacher assured her that such a thing could never happen, that parents want only what is best for their children. Later a school counselor in whom she confided eventually had sexual relations with her himself.

When I hear such stories, I could weep with frustration and sadness over a world that offers so little protection to its young.

Yet when I meet with the parents of these abused children, I most often come away feeling more sorrow than anger. Almost always they themselves have been abused as children. Their own frustrations and ineptness have isolated them from all the networks of friends or relatives that might help and monitor their behavior. They have little idea of what to expect from children and often violently overreact to a child's stubbornness or refusal to obey, even though other parents would have recognized the behavior as normal. I know a father who made a six-year-old son sit on his bed for six hours, refusing him food and forbidding him to go to the bathroom simply because he forgot to turn off his bedroom light after having been reminded. "You have to teach them to be responsible," he said. "If I'd forgotten to do what my dad told me, I'd have been hit with the buckle end of his belt. Let me tell you, my kid has it easy."

I'm not sure if there is more of this sort of thing occurring today than ever before. I am sure that our consciousness is raised in this matter. Many of us work very hard to help abusing parents learn new ways of handling problems with their children. And we work with the abused children themselves to help them handle their experience without passing it on to their own children.

QUESTION   As a counselor you must deal with all kinds of marital problems. Has there been any shift in what you see since the women's movement has challenged traditional roles?

C.B.   People are more up-front with some issues. The division of labor, for example. It used to be that people simply assumed they knew what men's and women's roles ought to be. When circumstances forced a change, couples became confused and annoyed, because it seldom occurred to them that there might be more than one way (the way they had grown up with) to look at the situation. Now everyone knows there are options. It's probably become easier to deal with since that's been taken for granted.

QUESTION   But aren't there problems that couples face today which simply wouldn't have come up a few years ago? For example, I have friends who are living hundreds of miles apart, not because they don't love each other but because they are a two-career family and their careers have led them to entirely different parts of the country.

C.B.   Well, that's one of the results of the increasing number of dual-career marriages. One partner gets an irresistible opportunity in another region, while the other is fully committed to the job he already has. An increasing number of couples simply decide to establish separate residences and try to keep the marriage alive by commuting. Sometimes it works; but it takes an incredible amount of energy, money, time and commitment. The pressures to move closer together, or to give up the marriage, are tremendous. I admire those who can make it work, but I could never do it myself. Even being away from home for three or four weeks drains my emotional reserves. I literally need—cannot function at peak levels without—the energy that comes from living with the person I love.

QUESTION   I think we are seeing more husbands who,

after several years of marriage, confess to their wives that they are gay. I suppose it happens the other way around too. What can a couple who love each other do in such a case?

C.B.   I do see couples who are faced with this issue. In my own experience it has mostly been the husband who is revealed to have been gay all those years. It makes a difference, though, how the revelation comes about. Often, the wife simply discovers his homosexual activities as another woman might find out about her husband's heterosexual affair. She may get a tip from a friend. She may find incriminating notes or overhear a telephone conversation. She may discover she has contracted a venereal disease and confront him with the fact. In such cases, there is not only the problem of the homosexuality itself but also resentment and the feeling of betrayal that is part of any infidelity.

It is substantially different when the gay partner comes to his wife and tells her that he loves her and has been struggling with a problem that has finally become too much for him to handle alone. He doesn't want to hurt her, but he feels she needs to know that he is gay. Often such scenes are tender. Tears are shed on both sides, and the couple work together on handling the problem without destroying their relationship.

All the things I said in the chapter on coping with heterosexual infidelity apply here. There is also another element. If a couple should agree that for them the solution is a renewed commitment to their relationship, with a forswearing on his part of all extramarital sexual activities, he may find it more difficult than would a man with a heterosexual involvement. In addition to detaching himself from a loving relationship with another person, he is likely to have to withdraw from a whole network of friends, from a covert life-style that may have been deeply valued and from a definition of himself as intrinsically and irreversibly gay.

We don't know much about what makes one person gay, another straight and a third capable of both kinds of attraction. It is my philosophy, however, that if the couple hope to survive, the gay partner has to accept not only the fact that he is homosexual but also that he is a free agent, capable at least of choosing what he will *do*, if not how he feels. There is a great deal of rhetoric in the gay movement to the effect that a person cannot and must not fight his own homosexual nature. I guess I believe that the fundamental human qualities of love, commitment, patience and loyalty have almost nothing to do with whether a person is homosexual or heterosexual. When a person is in touch with these basic qualities in himself, he can handle the other issues with more confidence.

I would not pretend that this is an easy issue to deal with, but I have seen a number of couples who have dealt compassionately and constructively with the challenge and have achieved a deeper and more satisfying marriage as a result.

QUESTION How about other special circumstances? I imagine, for example, that couples from different racial or religious or social backgrounds have special problems that others don't have to deal with.

C.B. All marriages are "mixed" to some degree; but it is true that those which involve people from greatly disparate cultures, races, faiths or ages have special difficulties to deal with. Yet in my experience with such couples, I'm impressed with how similar their problems are to everyone else's. The same skills are required to negotiate differences whether they be large or small. Outsiders may assume that the racial or religious issues must be preeminent in the mixed marriage. In reality, though, the partners are more likely to be concerned with sex or disciplining the children or money worries, as are most people.

QUESTION Let me ask a different kind of question. The other day I got a brochure inviting me to join a computer matchmaking program. The claim was made that it had helped thousands of people find suitable partners on the basis of scientific matching. As it happens, I'm already mated, but

I wondered what you thought about such programs. Are they as scientific as they say? Do you think they're helpful to those who, perhaps, don't find it easy to locate eligible partners? Is it just a commercial gimmick, or is there some substance to it?

C.B.   I have nothing against computers. In fact, for many years I wrote my own programs for processing the data collected in my research projects. But I cannot believe that computers will ever have much to offer to people looking for a mate. It seems to me that the courtship process requires an opportunity to check a person out in a casual setting before anyone's intentions are declared. Early contacts are often incidental; early dates are mostly for fun, not for real. I cannot help feeling that there is something stifling about two people's going out when each knows the other has paid several hundred dollars for the privilege and is anxious to get his money's worth. School, mutual frends, church socials, office parties, jobs, and even singles bars seem to me to have a potential for forming successful relationships that's superior to even the most sophisticated computer matching program. If some have been helped, I'm glad for them; but I would need convincing that it's a good investment generally.

QUESTION   One last question. I read an article some months ago recommending that couples go to a marriage counselor every year for a marital checkup, just as they would go for a physical checkup. Problems could be caught while they were still small and easier to deal with. Do you see a day when marriage counselors will take a preventive approach rather than wait until major problems are laid on their doorstep?

C.B.   Perhaps you will be surprised to learn that I take a different view of the matter. Basically, the argument you quote compares the marriage to the human body and the annual visit with a marriage counselor to a routine physical checkup. I realize that many of my colleagues in the profession would see that as a perfectly appropriate analogy.

I feel that a slightly different comparison comes closer to the reality I experience when I work with couples.

To me, the counselor who probes the internal workings of a marriage is more like a surgeon than a public-health nurse. The core of a good marriage is protected by an outer layer of loyalty and privacy. It is no small thing for a third person to intrude. I am not one to shrink from the knife if an operation is called for, but you won't catch me signing up for annual exploratory surgery just to make sure that everything is all right in there. It follows that when intervention is indicated, the goal should be to get in and get out as quickly and cleanly as possible. Some counselors seem to want to become a permanent artificial heart (or perhaps kidney?) for the marriage. To me, the goal is to return the couple to their own care and keeping as soon as possible and for as long as may be. If their first experience was a good one, they will be the best judges of whether and when they need to come back.

13

A CONSUMER'S GUIDE TO MARITAL AND SEXUAL COUNSELORS

At various points in the text I have suggested that if all else fails you might seek the help of a professional counselor. I am painfully aware, however, that in practice it may not be that easy to get good help.

Marriage "helpers" come in a bewildering number of guises. They come from many backgrounds, and represent differing schools of thought, both as to training and as to professional philosophy. Some of them will have personal values and styles that suit your own; others will not. The final criterion, however, is always effectiveness, pure and simple. In this final chapter, I want to look at these three areas—professional training, personal qualities and effectiveness—and try to give you some guidance in each.

TRAINING AND PROFESSIONAL AFFILIATION

Those who practice marriage, family and sex counseling vary tremendously in their professional preparation. Since this is a relatively new field, the edges are a bit fuzzy; but at least five different groups are sufficiently distinguishable to warrant separate mention. (They are ranked here in descending order of cost, rather than of competence.)

1. PSYCHIATRISTS

A psychiatrist is a medical doctor who specializes in treating individuals with emotional problems. As a physician, he can write prescriptions for tranquilizers or other medication. Most psychiatrists, however, have had little or no preparation for relationship counseling. Those who do specialize in this field have usually had special training and make excellent counselors. Their fees, though, generally run 50 to 100 percent higher than those of other groups. Therefore, you should know a proposed psychiatrist's professional background before you put your money down. Simply ask whether he has received specialized training in marriage, family or sexual counseling. If the answer is "no," then you should continue only if both you and your spouse agree that the problems you have as a couple are secondary to the emotional problems of one, or both, of you.

2. CLINICAL PSYCHOLOGISTS

Clinical psychologists usually have an academic doctoral degree (Ph.D.) but are not medical doctors. They are trained in testing and individual therapy—but, as in the case of psychiatrists, it should not be assumed that they are experts in relationship counseling unless they have received special training and supervision in this area. Again, it is wise to ask and proceed accordingly.

3. Marriage and Family Counselors

Those professionals may have a doctor's or master's degree; theoretically, they should be specialists in relationship counseling of all kinds. In actuality, they vary tremendously in their training. Only a few states require licensing in this field. In most states, anyone at all can hang out a shingle as a marriage counselor or family consultant. Where there is no licensing, it is particularly important to be sure that the therapist has clinical membership in one of the major professional associations such as the American Association of Marriage and Family Counselors (see page 220 for address).

4. Social Workers

Social workers may have doctorates, but are more likely to have Master of Social Work (MSW) degrees. The majority are employed in public agencies, but an increasing number are in private practice. As with the other relationship counselors listed, they differ in the amount of training they have received and should be interviewed as to their background in this area.

5. Pastoral Counselors

Ministers, priests and rabbis also vary widely when it comes to their training for relationship counseling. Their special advantages are that they often know intimately the families they counsel and share their values and symbols. Moreover, for members of their congregations they usually charge no fee. Those who have had no training in this area will sometimes make referrals to colleagues more competent than themselves.

Many other professionals are also involved in marital, family or sex counseling. Family physicians, gynecologists, school psychologists, lawyers, vocational counselors and others may try their hand at it. In every case, it is appropriate to ask what training (if any) they have received in this specialty.

If you live near a university where training in marriage

counseling is done, it may be possible to get good help at small cost from trainees under supervision. I, for example, direct such a clinic at the University of Southern California.

6. SEX COUNSELORS

There is a growing group of professionals who designate themselves as specialists in their area of sexual counseling. They range from highly trained sex therapists to "weekend wonders" (whose credentials consist of attendance at a weekend workshop). At present there is no state licensing in this field. The American Society for Sex Educators, Counselors and Therapists (ASSECT) has begun to establish standards and evaluate credentials, but training for sex counselors is still in its infancy.

PERSONAL QUALITIES

Counselors are people, and they differ, as all people do, in their personal values, in their life-styles and even in their moral integrity. It is important for you to select someone who has not only the highest principles in general, but also a personal style that matches your own. If you are basically reticent, for example, you need assurance that you will not be counseled to do things which offend your values (such as curse and yell at your spouse, join a touchy-feely group, take off your clothes in the office or have an affair). On the other hand, you may feel that these more flamboyant approaches are just what the doctor should order. In any case, you can improve your chances of finding the right counselor by seeking personal referrals and by not being afraid to "shop" for the best.

1. *Personal Referrals.* Choosing a doctor or a lawyer or a hairdresser simply out of the Yellow Pages is probably

foolish. The same is true in selecting a marriage counselor. If you have a friend or relative who has had good experiences with a particular counselor, consider that the best reference. In the absence of that kind of personal information, a good public reputation is the next-best recommendation. Ministers, doctors and lawyers often have occasion to refer people to counselors, and they can sometimes provide you with feedback as to whether real help was received. If none of these sources is available to you, consult a professional directory or even the telephone directory. Phone at least a half dozen counselors and ask them all some leading questions. Inquire, for example, whom they would go to if they had marital or sexual problems. Use any stratagem you like—but however you do it, find out as much as you can before committing yourself to a particular counselor.

2. *Shopping.* People who wouldn't think of buying a car from the first dealer they talked to, or buying a coat without shopping around, often feel strangely obliged to stick with the first counselor (or doctor, dentist or lawyer) they happen to go to. Part of the problem is that they feel relatively comfortable evaluating clothes or automobiles, but are at sea when it comes to professional help. I have two simple yardsticks which I suggest you apply to any counselor on the very first visit. They will quickly tell you whether you've got a bargain or a lemon.

    a. Does this person seem to understand and care how you feel; does he or she see clearly what is going on in the relationship; does he or she appear to "know the score"?

    b. Do this person's ideas make good common sense, or do they seem strange, dumb or outrageous?

If the counselor passes this test, make another appointment. If not, trust your own judgment and keep shopping until you find someone you can trust and work with.

THE EFFECTIVENESS OF THERAPY

Some forms of couple therapy are more effective than others. For example, counselors who make a point of dealing with couples as couples are successful about 75 percent of the time; those who prefer to see spouses separately, only about 50 percent. Of course, there are circumstances in which separate sessions are best; but the percentages suggest that this approach should be chosen only if there is some persuasive reason not to proceed as a pair.

The proof of the pudding is in the eating, however, and the final test of whether a particular counselor is right for you is whether, under his or her guidance, things start to improve. In my opinion, if improvements haven't begun to occur by the fourth weekly session, you have grounds for questioning whether you have the right combination of client and counselor. Of course, there are reasons other than incompetent counseling for getting stuck. Perhaps one partner is not ready to try, or perhaps the conflicting styles of couple and counselor keep them from working well together. Whatever the reason, if nothing good is happening, have the courage to quit.

Do not be intimidated by the strategy of certain counselors who imply that the real problem is your moral or religious hang-ups. Reject any diagnosis which suggests that unless you adopt the counselor's philosophy or life-style, you cannot be helped. You may, of course, choose to work on changing some attitude or inhibition yourself, if you decide that it stands between you and goals you have adopted. But don't be afraid to stand your ground if the counselor's requests violate your own values or standards. The best counselors will respect your position even if they do not share it.

Everyone is reluctant to admit failure; but when snags occur, ethical counselors will be willing to acknowledge that they are stuck and recommend colleagues who might work with you more successfully. If, therefore, you find your counselor hanging on to you even though he doesn't seem to be helping you much, exercise your consumer rights and switch.

It sometimes happens that a husband and wife can't agree on whether the counselor is effective or not. In such a case, the problem may be that the counselor is relating more warmly and supportively to one than to the other. If this is not corrected, the chances of success will be much reduced. In fact, my own philosophy is that the best marriage counseling views the relationship itself as the client rather than the individual partners. From this perspective, a lopsided approach just won't work and is a just ground for seeking a different counselor.

All of this probably makes finding a marriage counselor sound more hazardous than it really is. There are plenty of professionals who get excellent results. In fact, it is the very availability of so many solid counselors that makes it foolish to settle for one who is less than competent or who does not suit your personal style.

Places to Write for Qualified Relationship Counselors in Your Area:

> The American Association of Marriage and Family Counselors
> 225 Yale Avenue
> Claremont, California 91711 Phone: (714) 621-4749

For Specialists in Sexual Counseling:
> The American Association of Sex Educators, Counselors & Therapists
> 5010 Wisconsin Avenue, N.W., Suite 304
> Washington, D.C. 20015 Phone: (202) 686-2523

EPILOGUE

When something goes wrong with a marriage, the most appealing diagnosis, as I have often noted, is that the cause is a spouse's character defects. This book is dedicated to an alternative view of the matter. I believe that marriages mostly suffer in morale because 1) they are in competition with jobs and children and houses and hobbies and the rest of life for limited resources and 2) even when resources are committed to the marriage the results may be disappointing. I suppose neither this nor any other book can do much about the first problem. Life *is* demanding, and a couple have to allot their limited resources as best they can among a number of competing pressures. But I have tried to deal with the second problem to the best of my ability.

Nothing is more discouraging than to invest scarce energy and dwindling morale in a genuine effort to improve a relationship and have nothing change or things get even worse. I have come to believe that very often the failure is due to ignorance of the principles that govern success in human relationships. Given some residual spark of life and the motivation to succeed, I believe that attention to emotional space and noncompetitive communication and the unhooking of vicious circles and all the rest will actually work. Even a wretchedly bedraggled, undernourished marriage can be nurtured back to health. I have seen it happen over and over again; but I never lose my sense of awe and satisfaction at the results. Few things in life bring a richer return on one's investment.

REFERENCES

Beck, Dorothy F. "Research Findings on the Outcomes of Marriage Counseling in Olsen," David H. L. Olsen, ed. *Treating Relationships*, Lake Mills, Iowa: Graphic Publishing Company, 1976.

Broderick, Carlfred B. "Fathers," *The Family Coordinator*, 26:269–275 (1977), Minneapolis: National Council on Family Relations.

Cuber, J. F., and Peggy B. Harroff. *The Significant Americans*. New York: Appleton-Century-Crofts, 1965.

Duberman, Lucile. *The Reconstituted Family: A Study of Remarried Couples and Their Children*. Chicago: Nelson-Hall Publishers, 1975.

Ellis, Albert. *Growth Through Reason*. Palo Alto: Science and Behavior Books, 1971.

Erikson, Erik. *Childhood and Society*. New York: W. W. Norton & Company, Inc., 1950.

Kegel, A. H. "Sexual Functions of the Pubococcygens Muscle," *Western Journal of Surgery*, 60:521–524, 1952.

Masters, William, and Virginia Johnson. *Human Sexual Inadequacy*. Boston: Little, Brown & Company, 1970.

Overstreet, Harry and Bonaro. *The Mind Alive*. New York: W. W. Norton and Company, Inc., 1954.

————. *The Mind Goes Forth.* New York: W. W. Norton and Company, Inc., 1956.

Semans, J. H. "Premature Ejaculation: A New Approach," *Southern Medical Journal,* 49: 353–358, 1956.

Stuart, Richard B. "An Operant Interpersonal Program for Couples," David H. L. Olsen, ed. *Treating Relationships,* Lake Mills, Iowa: Graphic Publishing Company, 1976.